THE CASSEROLE COOKBOOK

Jackie Johnson & the Culinary Arts Staff
Illustrations: Justin Wager
Photographs: Zdenek Pivecka

Culinary Arts Institute®
A DIVISION OF DELAIR PUBLISHING COMPANY

CONTENTS

Cover photo: He-Man Casserole, 25

Library of Congress Catalog Card Number: 79-51592
ISBN: 0-8326-0617-0

INTRODUCTION

Casseroles have become synonymous with one-dish cooking, but casseroles can also be easy, budget-wise, time-efficient, and delicious. Casserole cookery is combining foods in one dish and baking it. The result is a flavorful combination of the ingredients.

Casseroles can be served as an appealing appetizer, a hearty main dish, a delightfully different brunch, an interesting pasta, grain, or vegetable side dish, and as an elegant dessert. Casseroles can be incorporated into your meals in many sizes, shapes, and forms.

It can't be denied that casseroles are easy to prepare. In many recipes, all the raw ingredients are combined in an oven-proof dish, put in the oven, and the cook is freed from the kitchen, only to come back to serve the food. Cleanup is easy, too, since there is only one dish to wash instead of several pots and pans. And if there are leftovers, they can be stored in the refrigerator in the same dish and then later popped in the oven for quick reheating.

Some recipes require an ingredient to be cooked on top of the range first, combined with the other ingredients, and then cooked in the oven. This extra step in casserole cookery is worth that little bit of effort since it improves the flavor of the casserole.

Casseroles with ground meat require that the meat be cooked first to assure that it is thoroughly cooked, and drained to avoid grease in the final product.

And talk about ground beef! Casseroles are a great way of serving ground beef, a budget food of many families today. In this book, you'll find enough ground beef casseroles to prepare for a month and

never duplicate a meal. Casseroles are an excellent means of stretching the food dollar. A pound of meat usually serves four, but in a casserole, that pound of meat can serve up to six people.

Main-dish casseroles are also an appealing way of obtaining balanced nutrition. Since meats are often combined with cheese, noodles, or vegetables, you can be assured that the people at the dinner table are consuming many necessary vitamins and minerals.

When you are entertaining, casseroles are heaven-sent. Many dishes can be prepared hours ahead of time, stored in the refrigerator, and put in the oven when the guests arrive. In this way, you spend time with your guests and not in the kitchen. And if for some reason dinner is delayed, the casserole can be kept warm in the oven and still maintain its freshness. Casseroles are perfect on a buffet table too, because of their ease in serving.

Casseroles aren't a new way of cooking; however, the CULINARY ARTS INSTITUTE® has improved the concept of one-dish cooking. All recipes have been kitchen-tested, so you can be confident that each recipe will be successful.

Casseroles are the answer for the cook in a hurry, for those on a budget, for those with unexpected guests, and for cooks who enjoy diversification.

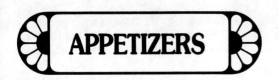

If you need a delicious but easy appetizer for that special dinner, look no further. In this chapter you'll find ideas for all kinds of appetizers from elegant Crab Meat Quiche to crowd-pleaser Barbecue Fondue. All you have to do is combine the ingredients, pop the dish in the oven, and your guests will eat it up. *Bon appetit!*

Hot Crab Spread

1 package (8 ounces) cream cheese, softened
1 tablespoon milk
2 teaspoons Worcestershire sauce
1 can (7½ ounces) Alaska King crab, drained and flaked, or 1 package (6 ounces) frozen crab meat, thawed, drained, and flaked
2 tablespoons chopped green onion
2 tablespoons toasted slivered almonds

1. Combine cream cheese, milk, Worcestershire sauce, crab, and green onion. Place in small individual casseroles. Sprinkle with almonds.
2. Bake, uncovered, at 350°F 15 minutes. Serve with **assorted crackers.**

2 cups

Crab Meat Newburg Appetizer

2 tablespoons butter or margarine
2 tablespoons flour
½ teaspoon salt
2 cups milk
2 cups (8 ounces) shredded Cheddar cheese
2 cans (7½ ounces each) Alaska King crab, drained and flaked
3 hard-cooked eggs, grated
½ cup finely chopped onion
Dash ground red pepper
1 tablespoon snipped parsley

1. Melt butter in a saucepan. Add flour and salt. Gradually add milk, stirring until thickened and smooth.
2. Add cheese, stirring until blended. Blend in remaining ingredients, except parsley. Put into a 1½-quart casserole.
3. Bake, covered, at 325°F 15 minutes, or until heated through. Sprinkle with parsley. Serve with **Melba toast** or **toast-points.**

25 servings

Crab Meat Quiche

1 unbaked 9-inch pie shell
2 eggs
1 cup half-and-half
½ teaspoon salt
Dash ground red pepper
¾ cup (3 ounces) shredded Swiss cheese
¾ cup (3 ounces) shredded Gruyère cheese
1 tablespoon flour
1 can (7½ ounces) Alaska King crab, drained and flaked

1. Prick bottom and sides of pie shell. Bake at 450°F 10 minutes, or until delicately browned.
2. Beat together eggs, half-and-half, salt, and red pepper.
3. Combine cheeses, flour, and crab; sprinkle evenly in pie shell. Pour in egg mixture.
4. Bake, uncovered, at 325°F 45 minutes, or until tip of knife inserted 1 inch from center comes out clean. Let stand a few minutes. Cut into wedges to serve.

16 appetizers

Barbecue Fondue

2 cans (15¼ ounces each) barbecue
    sauce and beef for Sloppy Joes
1 teaspoon instant minced onion
1 teaspoon oregano
1½ cups (6 ounces) shredded Cheddar
    cheese

1. Combine all ingredients in a 1-quart casserole.
2. Bake, covered, at 350°F 30 minutes, or until heated through, stirring occasionally. Serve with **French bread cubes** on wooden picks.

3½ cups

Mexican Chili-Bean Dip

1 pound ground beef
½ cup finely chopped onion
½ cup ketchup
1 tablespoon chili powder
1 teaspoon salt
⅛ teaspoon garlic powder
    Dash ground red pepper
1 can (15½ ounces) red kidney beans
    (with liquid), mashed
1 cup (4 ounces) shredded Monterey
    Jack cheese

1. Brown ground beef and onion in a skillet; drain off excess fat.
2. Add remaining ingredients, except cheese. Put into a 1-quart casserole.
3. Bake, covered, at 350°F 30 minutes, or until heated through. Sprinkle with cheese. Serve with **corn chips.**

8 servings

Hot Artichoke-Cheese Squares

¼ cup finely chopped onion
1 garlic clove, minced
1 tablespoon shortening
4 eggs, well beaten
1 can (14 ounces) artichoke hearts,
    drained and chopped
¼ cup dry bread crumbs
2 cups (8 ounces) shredded Cheddar
    or Swiss cheese
2 tablespoons snipped parsley
    Few drops Tabasco

1. Sauté onion and garlic in shortening in a skillet.
2. Combine all ingredients. Pour into an 11x7-inch baking dish.
3. Bake, uncovered, at 325°F 30 minutes, or until filling is set. Let stand a few minutes. Cut into squares to serve.

24 appetizers

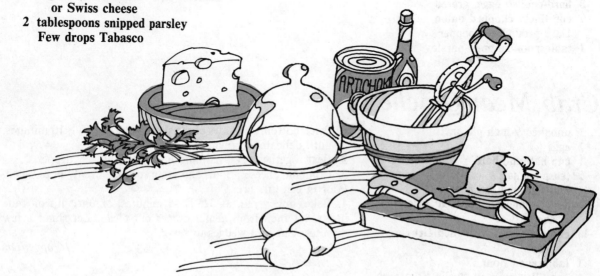

Sausage and Applesauce Appetizers

1 package (12 ounces) smoked link
    sausage, cut in 1-inch pieces
1 jar (15 ounces) applesauce
1 tablespoon caraway seed
1½ teaspoons instant minced onion

1. Broil sausage pieces until evenly browned.
2. Combine with applesauce, caraway seed, and onion. Put into a 1-quart casserole.
3. Bake, covered, at 250°F 2 hours. Serve with wooden picks.

About 32 appetizers

Baked Carrot Spread

1 cup grated carrot
1 cup mayonnaise
1 cup (4 ounces) grated Romano
    cheese
½ teaspoon garlic salt
½ teaspoon lemon pepper seasoning

1. Combine all ingredients in a 1-quart casserole.
2. Bake, uncovered, at 350°F 25 minutes, or until heated through. Serve with **assorted crackers.**

3 cups

Baked Mushrooms

1½ pounds fresh mushroom caps*
1 cup butter or margarine, melted
2 teaspoons finely chopped onion
1 garlic clove, minced
½ teaspoon rosemary
¾ teaspoon Worcestershire sauce

1. Place mushroom caps in a 1½-quart casserole.
2. Combine remaining ingredients. Pour over mushrooms.
3. Bake, covered, at 325°F 30 minutes, or until tender.

12 servings

* The mushroom stems can be sautéed and added to **hot, cooked green beans.**

Onion Appetizers

4 medium onions, finely chopped
3 tablespoons butter or margarine
½ cup dairy sour cream
1 tablespoon flour
½ teaspoon salt
    Dash pepper
1 teaspoon caraway seed
3 eggs, beaten
4 bacon slices, cooked and crumbled
1 unbaked 9-inch pie shell

1. Sauté onion in butter in a skillet.
2. Blend sour cream, flour, salt, pepper, and caraway seed. Beat in eggs. Stir in bacon and onion. Pour into pie shell.
3. Bake, uncovered, at 325°F 35 to 40 minutes, or until filling is set. Let stand a few minutes. Cut into wedges to serve.

16 appetizers

MEAT

Main-dish casseroles appeal to our common sense because they are easy, economical, nutritious, and flavorful. The whole meal can be mixed, baked, and served in one dish, giving the cook more freedom. You'll find recipes here using many varieties of meat from ground beef to pork chops. Ground beef is especially versatile in casseroles, and it lets you stretch the food to serve more people. And when combined with other foods, meat casseroles acquire a special character and new flavors for your family to enjoy at mealtime.

Taco Casserole

1 **pound ground beef**
1 **package (1.25 ounces) taco seasoning mix**
1 **cup water**
1 **can (15 ounces) refried beans with sausage**
2 **cups shredded lettuce**
¼ **cup chopped onion**
1 **tablespoon chopped green chilies**
1 **cup (4 ounces) shredded Cheddar cheese**
  Nacho-flavored tortilla chips
  Chopped tomato
  Sliced ripe olives
  Dairy sour cream
  Taco sauce

1. Brown ground beef in a skillet; drain off excess fat. Add taco mix and water. Simmer, uncovered, until mixture is thickened (about 15 minutes).
2. Lightly grease bottom of an 11x7-inch baking dish. Spread refried beans evenly on the bottom. Sprinkle with shredded lettuce, onion, and chilies; top with ground beef mixture. (If desired, cover and refrigerate until ready to finish.)
3. Bake, uncovered, at 400°F 15 minutes. Sprinkle with shredded cheese and bake an additional 5 minutes, or until cheese is melted and mixture is heated through.
4. Remove from oven and garnish with tortilla chips.
5. Serve with chopped tomato, sliced olives, sour cream, and taco sauce in separate serving dishes.

6 servings

Savannah Beef and Noodles

1 **pound ground beef**
1 **cup chopped onion**
1 **can (28 ounces) tomatoes (undrained)**
2 **teaspoons salt**
2 **teaspoons chili powder**
1 **teaspoon Worcestershire sauce**
3 **cups cooked noodles**
1 **can (5¾ ounces) pitted ripe olives, sliced**
2 **cups (8 ounces) shredded Cheddar cheese**

1. Brown ground beef and onion in a skillet; drain off excess fat. Add tomatoes, salt, chili powder, and Worcestershire sauce; simmer 30 minutes.
2. Alternate layers of half the noodles, half the meat mixture, and half the ripe olives in a 2½-quart casserole; repeat layers. Top with shredded cheese.
3. Bake, covered, at 350°F 30 minutes, or until heated through.

6 to 8 servings

Easy Beefy Casserole

- **1 pound ground beef**
- **2 cans (16 ounces each) tomatoes (undrained)**
- **1 can (16 ounces) whole kernel corn, drained**
- **¼ cup sliced stuffed olives**
- **½ cup chopped green pepper**
- **1 teaspoon oregano**
- **1½ tablespoons instant minced onion**
- **1 teaspoon salt**
- **½ teaspoon pepper**
- **2 cups (about 4 ounces) uncooked noodles**
- **¼ cup (1 ounce) grated Parmesan cheese**

1. Brown ground beef in a skillet; drain off excess fat. Add remaining ingredients, except cheese. Put into a 2-quart casserole.
2. Bake, covered, at 350°F 25 minutes. Remove cover. Sprinkle with grated cheese and bake an additional 5 minutes, or until heated through.

6 servings

Baked Steak Patties

- **1 pound ground beef**
- **½ pound pork sausage meat**
- **2 cups cooked white rice**
- **1 egg**
- **6 bacon slices**
- **1 package (1⅜ ounces) dry onion soup mix**
- **3 cups water**
- **2 tablespoons flour**

1. Combine ground beef, sausage, rice, and egg. Shape to form 6 patties. Wrap each with a bacon slice; secure with wooden pick. Place in an 11x7-inch baking dish.
2. Bake, uncovered, at 350°F 30 minutes; drain off excess fat.
3. Meanwhile, combine soup mix and 2½ cups water in a saucepan. Cook, covered, 10 minutes.
4. Mix the remaining ½ cup water and flour until smooth. Gradually add to soup mixture, stirring until thickened.
5. Pour over steak patties and bake an additional 20 minutes. Remove picks before serving.

6 servings

Note: The gravy may be served with the steak patties or covered and refrigerated. Reheat and serve with mashed potatoes at the next evening's meal.

Party Beef Casserole

  2 **pounds ground beef**
  ¾ **cup chopped onion**
  1 **garlic clove, minced**
  ½ **cup chopped green pepper**
  ½ **cup chopped celery**
  1 **teaspoon salt**
  ½ **teaspoon pepper**
  1 **can (15 ounces) tomato sauce**
  1 **can (8 ounces) mushroom stems and pieces, drained**
  1 **can (6 ounces) tomato paste**
  ½ **cup sherry**
  2 **tablespoons Worcestershire sauce**
  1 **package (7 ounces) shell macaroni, cooked and drained**
  1 **cup (4 ounces) shredded Cheddar cheese**

1. Brown ground beef, onion, garlic, green pepper, and celery in a skillet; drain off excess fat. Combine with remaining ingredients, except shredded cheese. Put into a 3-quart casserole.
2. Bake, covered, at 350°F 45 minutes. Sprinkle with shredded cheese and bake an additional 5 minutes, or until heated through.

8 to 10 servings

Spanish Take-Along Casserole

  1½ **pounds ground beef**
  ½ **cup chopped onion**
  ¼ **cup chopped green pepper**
  ¼ **cup chopped celery**
  1 **can (8 ounces) pizza sauce**
  2 **cups (about 4 ounces) medium noodles, cooked and drained**
  1 **teaspoon salt**
  1 **carton (16 ounces) cream-style cottage cheese**

1. Brown ground beef, onion, green pepper, and celery in a skillet; drain off excess fat. Combine with remaining ingredients.
2. Put into a 2-quart casserole. (If desired, cover and refrigerate until ready to finish.)
3. Bake, covered, at 350°F 30 minutes, or until heated through. Garnish with **green pepper rings.**

6 to 8 servings

Super Macaroni and Beef Bake

1 package (6 ounces) elbow macaroni
1 package (8 ounces) cream cheese
1 carton (16 ounces) cream-style cottage cheese
¼ cup dairy sour cream
1½ pounds ground beef
3 cans (8 ounces each) tomato sauce
½ cup (2 ounces) grated Parmesan cheese

1. Cook macaroni in **boiling salted water** until just tender; rinse with cold water. Place half the macaroni in bottom of a greased 13x9-inch baking dish.
2. With mixer beat together cream cheese, cottage cheese, and sour cream; pour over macaroni. Sprinkle remaining macaroni over cheese mixture.
3. Brown ground beef in a skillet; drain off excess fat. Stir in tomato sauce. Evenly spread meat mixture over macaroni. Sprinkle with grated cheese.
4. Bake, uncovered, at 350°F 50 to 60 minutes, or until heated through.

8 servings

Note: This casserole is best when prepared a day in advance. Cover and refrigerate. Remove from refrigerator 1 hour before baking.

Italian Spaghetti Bake

1 pound ground beef
½ cup chopped onion
1 can (16 ounces) tomatoes, drained
1 can (6 ounces) tomato paste
1 garlic clove, minced
1½ teaspoons salt
½ teaspoon oregano
½ teaspoon basil
¼ teaspoon whole marjoram
1 package (7 ounces) spaghetti
2 cups milk
3 eggs
  Dash of pepper
1 cup (4 ounces) grated Parmesan cheese
1 cup (4 ounces) shredded mozzarella cheese

1. Brown ground beef and onion in a skillet; drain off excess fat. Stir in tomatoes, tomato paste, garlic, 1 teaspoon salt, oregano, basil, and marjoram.
2. Cook spaghetti in **boiling salted water** until just tender. Spread in bottom of a 13x9-inch baking dish.
3. Combine milk, eggs, pepper, and remaining ½ teaspoon salt. Pour over spaghetti. Sprinkle with Parmesan cheese. Spoon meat mixture over Parmesan cheese. Top with mozzarella cheese.
4. Bake, uncovered, at 350°F 40 to 45 minutes, or until heated through. Let stand 10 minutes. Cut into squares to serve.

8 servings

Lasagne Bolognese

3 tablespoons butter or margarine
3 tablespoons flour
1 cup milk
1 cup whipping cream
¼ teaspoon salt
Dash of pepper
½ pound lasagne noodles
Meat Sauce Bolognese
1 cup (4 ounces) grated Parmesan cheese

1. Melt butter in a saucepan; blend in flour. Gradually add milk and cream, stirring until thickened and smooth. Add salt and pepper.
2. Cook lasagne noodles in **boiling salted water** according to package directions. Drain, rinse, and spread on a damp towel.
3. Spread a thin layer of Meat Sauce Bolognese in a 13x9-inch baking dish. Top with a layer of half the lasagne noodles, half the Meat Sauce Bolognese, half the white sauce, and half the cheese; repeat layers.
4. Bake, uncovered, at 375°F 35 to 40 minutes, or until mixture is bubbly and top is golden brown. Let stand 10 minutes. Cut into squares to serve.

8 servings

Meat Sauce Bolognese

6 bacon slices, diced
1 medium onion, chopped
½ cup chopped celery
½ cup chopped carrot
6 tablespoons butter or margarine
¼ pound chicken livers, diced
1 pound ground beef round
1 teaspoon salt
½ teaspoon oregano
¼ teaspoon nutmeg
1 bay leaf
2 tablespoons vinegar
1 can (8 ounces) tomato sauce
1 cup beef bouillon
1 cup sliced fresh mushrooms
½ cup dry white wine

1. Sauté bacon in a skillet; drain off all but 2 tablespoons fat. Add onion, celery, and carrot; cook until tender.
2. Add 2 tablespoons butter and the chicken livers. Brown lightly; add ground beef round. Cook 10 to 15 minutes, or until well browned.
3. Stir in salt, oregano, nutmeg, bay leaf, vinegar, tomato sauce, and bouillon. Cover and simmer ½ hour.
4. Sauté mushrooms in remaining 4 tablespoons butter. Add to meat sauce along with wine. Remove bay leaf. Simmer ½ hour longer.

1 quart

Beef and Pea Casserole

1 pound ground beef
1 medium onion, chopped
1 can (10¾ ounces) condensed tomato soup
⅓ cup water
2 cups cooked noodles
1 can (8 ounces) peas, drained*
1 can (4 ounces) sliced mushrooms, drained*

1. Brown ground beef and onion in a skillet; drain off excess fat. Combine with remaining ingredients. Put into a 2-quart casserole.
2. Bake, covered, at 350°F 30 minutes, or until heated through. To serve, sprinkle with **Parmesan cheese** and garnish with **pimento strips.**

6 servings

* The liquid from the peas or mushrooms may be substituted for the 1/3 cup water.

Cheese, Beef, 'n' Macaroni Bake

2 pounds ground beef
½ medium onion, chopped
1 garlic clove, minced
1 jar (15½ ounces) spaghetti sauce
1 can (16 ounces) stewed tomatoes
1 can (3 ounces) mushroom stems and
   pieces, drained
2 cups uncooked large macaroni
   shells
2 cups dairy sour cream
1 package (6 ounces) provolone
   cheese slices
1 cup (4 ounces) shredded mozzarella
   cheese

1. Brown ground beef in a skillet; drain off excess fat. Add onion, garlic, spaghetti sauce, tomatoes, and mushrooms. Mix well and simmer 20 minutes.
2. Meanwhile, prepare macaroni shells according to package directions.
3. Put the macaroni shells into a 3-quart casserole. Cover with half the meat sauce. Spread meat with half the sour cream. Top with provolone cheese.
4. Repeat macaroni, meat, and sour-cream layers. Top with mozzarella cheese.
5. Bake, covered, at 350°F 35 to 40 minutes. Remove cover. Bake an additional 10 minutes, or until cheese is lightly browned.

8 to 10 servings

Mock Chop Suey Casserole

1 pound ground beef
¾ cup chopped onion
2 cups chopped celery
1 can (10¾ ounces) condensed
   cream of chicken soup
1 can (10¾ ounces) condensed
   cream of mushroom soup
½ cup uncooked white rice
2 cups boiling water
1 tablespoon soy sauce
1 can (5 ounces) chow mein noodles

1. Brown ground beef in a skillet; drain off excess fat. Combine with remaining ingredients, except chow mein noodles. Put into a 13x9-inch baking dish.
2. Bake, covered, at 350°F 45 minutes, or until rice is tender. Uncover; sprinkle with chow mein noodles. Bake an additional 10 minutes, or until noodles are heated through.

6 servings

Beef and Rice Bake

1 pound ground beef
1 package (1⅜ ounces) dry onion
   soup mix
¾ cup uncooked white rice
1½ cups boiling water
1 can (16 ounces) tomatoes
   (undrained)
1 cup (4 ounces) shredded Cheddar
   cheese

1. Brown ground beef in a skillet; drain off excess fat. Combine with soup mix, rice, boiling water, and tomatoes. Put into a 2-quart casserole.
2. Bake, covered, at 350°F 45 minutes, or until rice is tender. Uncover; sprinkle with cheese. Bake an additional 5 minutes, or until cheese is melted.

6 servings

Easy Meatball Stroganoff

1 tablespoon instant minced onion
½ cup milk
1½ pounds ground beef
⅔ cup quick or old-fashioned oats,
   uncooked
1 teaspoon salt
¼ teaspoon pepper
¼ teaspoon dill weed
⅛ teaspoon garlic powder
1 egg, beaten
1 can (10¾ ounces) condensed golden
   mushroom soup
½ cup dairy sour cream

1. Combine onion and milk. Mix ground beef, oats, salt, pepper, dill weed, garlic powder, egg, and onion-milk mixture.
2. Shape to form 24 meatballs. Place in a shallow 10-inch casserole. Spoon soup over meatballs.
3. Bake, covered, at 350°F 35 minutes, or until meatballs are cooked through, stirring occasionally.
4. Uncover; blend in sour cream. Serve over **hot, cooked rice.**

6 servings

Sloppy Joe for a Crowd

2¼ pounds ground beef
2½ cups chopped onion
1 cup chopped green pepper
1 bottle (14 ounces) ketchup
¼ cup firmly packed brown sugar
¼ cup lemon juice
¼ cup vinegar
¼ cup water
2 teaspoons salt
1 teaspoon pepper
1 teaspoon Worcestershire sauce
½ teaspoon prepared mustard

1. Brown ground beef, onion, and green pepper in a skillet; drain off excess fat. Combine with remaining ingredients. Put into a large oven-proof Dutch oven.
2. Bake, covered, at 325°F 1½ hours. To serve, spoon over **toasted hamburger buns.**

16 servings

Beef-Sour Cream Casserole

4 cups cooked noodles
1 cup (8 ounces) cream-style cottage
    cheese
1 package (8 ounces) cream cheese
¼ cup dairy sour cream
⅓ cup instant minced onion
2 tablespoons butter or margarine,
    melted
1½ pounds ground beef
3 cans (8 ounces each) tomato sauce
½ teaspoon salt
1 teaspoon oregano
⅓ cup chopped green pepper
1 can (2 ounces) sliced mushrooms,
    drained

1. Put half the noodles into a 2-quart casserole.
2. Combine cottage cheese, cream cheese, sour cream, and onion. Spread over noodles. Cover with remaining noodles. Drizzle with butter.
3. Brown ground beef in a skillet; drain off excess fat. Add remaining ingredients. Pour over noodles. Cover and chill overnight.
4. Remove from refrigerator 1 hour before baking.
5. Bake, covered, at 375°F 45 minutes, or until heated through. To serve, sprinkle with **grated Parmesan cheese.**

8 servings

Biscuit-Topped Burger

1¼ pounds ground beef
3 tablespoons instant minced onion
½ cup chopped celery
1 can (8 ounces) tomato sauce
2 tablespoons sweet pickle relish
½ teaspoon chili powder
½ teaspoon horseradish
¼ teaspoon salt
1 can (10 ounces) refrigerator biscuits
1 cup (4 ounces) shredded Cheddar
    cheese
1 tablespoon snipped parsley
½ teaspoon celery seed

1. Brown ground beef, onion, and celery in a skillet; drain off excess fat. Add tomato sauce, pickle relish, chili powder, horseradish, and salt. Simmer 2 minutes, or until heated through.
2. Spoon into an 11x7-inch baking dish.
3. Separate biscuits; then split each biscuit into 2 layers. Place half the biscuit halves over the meat mixture.
4. Combine cheese, parsley, and celery seed. Sprinkle over biscuit layer. Top with remaining biscuit halves.
5. Bake, uncovered, at 375°F 20 to 25 minutes, or until golden brown.

5 servings

Texas Chili

2 pounds ground beef
2 medium onions, chopped
1 garlic clove, minced
3 tablespoons flour
2 tablespoons chili powder
2 teaspoons salt
½ teaspoon cumin
3 cups hot water
1 can (15½ ounces) kidney beans,
　 drained

1. Brown ground beef, onion, and garlic in a skillet; drain off excess fat.
2. Combine flour, chili powder, salt, and cumin. Gradually stir in hot water. Combine with meat mixture. Pour into a 2½-quart casserole.
3. Bake, covered, at 350°F 1¼ hours. Remove cover. Add beans and bake an additional 15 minutes.

8 servings

Hominy-Beef Bake

2 pounds ground beef
3 medium onions, chopped
1 can (16 ounces) tomatoes
　 (undrained)
1 can (16 ounces) whole white
　 hominy, drained
1 can (16 ounces) whole kernel corn,
　 drained
1 can (16 ounces) cream-style corn
1 cup sliced pitted ripe olives
2 cans (8 ounces each) tomato sauce
1 package (1.25 ounces) chili mix
1 package (6 ounces) corn tortillas,
　 cut up

1. Brown ground beef and onion in a skillet; drain off excess fat.
2. Combine with remaining ingredients. Put into a 4-quart casserole.
3. Bake, covered, at 300°F 2 hours.

12 servings

Individual Burger Casseroles

1 pound ground beef
¼ cup finely chopped onion
1 teaspoon salt
¼ teaspoon oregano
2 tablespoons ketchup
1 cup plus 2 tablespoons milk
2 tablespoons butter or margarine
2 tablespoons flour
1 cup cooked mixed vegetables
2 slices American cheese, cut in 4
　 strips each

1. Combine ground beef, onion, ½ teaspoon salt, oregano, ketchup, and 2 tablespoons milk.
2. Divide into 4 equal portions. Evenly line bottom and sides of 4 individual casseroles with meat mixture.
3. Bake, uncovered, at 350°F 20 minutes, or until meat mixture is done. Pour off excess fat.
4. Meanwhile, melt butter in a saucepan. Stir in flour. Gradually add remaining 1 cup milk, stirring until thickened and smooth.
5. Add vegetables and remaining ½ teaspoon salt. Spoon into meat shells. Top each with crisscross of cheese strips.
6. Bake about 5 minutes or until cheese melts.

4 servings

African Bobotie

3 slices day-old bread
1½ cups milk
2 medium onions, chopped
1 garlic clove, minced
½ cup slivered almonds
½ cup raisins
1 tablespoon sugar
1 teaspoon salt
1 teaspoon curry powder
⅛ teaspoon pepper
1 tablespoon vinegar
1 teaspoon lemon juice
1½ pounds ground beef
2 eggs

1. Soak bread in milk. Squeeze milk from bread, reserving milk. Combine all ingredients, except milk and 1 egg.
2. Press mixture into an 11x7-inch baking dish.
3. Add enough milk to reserved milk to make ¾ cup. Beat together milk and remaining egg. Pour over meat mixture.
4. Bake, uncovered, at 350°F 1 hour, or until golden brown and firm to the touch.

6 servings

Mediterranean Beef Casserole

1 can (20 ounces) pineapple chunks
1 cup uncooked white rice
1 teaspoon salt
1 pound ground beef
1 egg, lightly beaten
1 cup fine soft bread crumbs
1 tablespoon instant minced onion
1 teaspoon salt
⅓ cup milk
1 tablespoon vegetable oil
1 can (16 ounces) stewed tomatoes
½ teaspoon dill weed
2 tablespoons snipped parsley

1. Drain pineapple, reserving liquid. Add enough **water** to liquid to make 2½ cups.
2. Combine liquid, rice, and 1 teaspoon of the salt in a saucepan. Bring to a boil. Cover and simmer 25 minutes, or until rice is fluffy.
3. Combine ground beef, egg, bread crumbs, onion, 1 teaspoon salt, and milk. Shape to form 1-inch balls.
4. Brown meatballs in oil in skillet; drain off excess fat.
5. Add pineapple chunks, tomatoes, dill weed, and parsley. Put into a greased 2-quart casserole.
6. Bake, covered, at 375°F 25 minutes, or until meat is done. Serve over pineapple-rice.

6 servings

Taco Casserole, 8

One 'n' One Casserole

1 pound ground beef
1 cup uncooked white rice
1 package (1⅜ ounces) dry onion
    soup mix
1 can (10¾ ounces) condensed cream
    of mushroom soup
2½ cups boiling water
½ cup sliced green onion tops

1. Brown ground beef in a skillet; drain off excess fat. Put into a greased 2-quart casserole. Sprinkle with rice and onion soup mix.
2. Combine mushroom soup and boiling water. Pour over rice.
3. Bake, covered, at 350°F 1 hour, or until rice is tender. Remove cover. Sprinkle with onion tops.

4 servings

Meatball Supper Pie

1 pound ground beef
½ cup quick or old-fashioned oats,
    uncooked
¼ cup chopped onion
1 teaspoon salt
¼ teaspoon pepper
¼ teaspoon thyme
1¼ cups milk
1 egg, beaten
1 tablespoon butter or margarine
1 tablespoon flour
    Dash ground red pepper
½ cup (2 ounces) grated Parmesan
    cheese
1 baked 9-inch pie shell
½ cup (2 ounces) shredded American
    cheese
1 tomato, cut in wedges

1. Combine ground beef, oats, onion, salt, pepper, thyme, ¼ cup milk, and egg. Shape to form 4 dozen small meatballs.
2. Brown meatballs in a skillet; drain off excess fat.
3. Melt butter in a saucepan. Stir in flour and red pepper. Gradually add remaining 1 cup milk, stirring until thickened and smooth. Stir in Parmesan cheese.
4. Place meatballs in pie shell. Pour cheese sauce over meatballs.
5. Bake, uncovered, at 375°F 20 minutes. Sprinkle with American cheese and top with tomato wedges. Bake an additional 5 minutes. Cut into wedges to serve.

6 servings

Layered Hamburger Bake

1 **pound ground beef**
1 **medium onion, chopped**
4 **medium potatoes, pared and sliced**
¼ **teaspoon pepper**
1 **can (10½ ounces) condensed vegetable soup**
1 **can (10¾ ounces) condensed cream of mushroom soup**
½ **cup water**

1. Brown ground beef and onion in a skillet; drain off excess fat.
2. Put half of the potatoes into a greased 2-quart casserole. Top with half the meat mixture; repeat. Sprinkle with pepper.
3. Combine vegetable soup, mushroom soup, and water. Pour over meat.
4. Bake, covered, at 350°F 1 hour, or until potatoes are tender.

4 servings

Tamale Pie

1 **cup cornmeal**
1¾ **teaspoons salt**
1 **cup cold water**
2 **cups boiling water**
1 **pound ground beef**
⅓ **cup chopped onion**
2 **tablespoons flour**
½ **cup chopped pitted ripe olives**
1 **can (16 ounces) tomatoes (undrained)**
2 **teaspoons chili powder**
½ **cup cubed sharp Cheddar cheese**

1. Combine cornmeal, 1 teaspoon salt, and cold water. Slowly pour into boiling water in a saucepan, stirring constantly. Cook until thickened, stirring frequently. Cover; continue cooking over low heat about 5 minutes. Stir occasionally.
2. Brown ground beef and onion in a skillet; drain off excess fat. Add flour, olives, tomatoes, chili powder, and remaining ¾ teaspoon salt.
3. Spread mush evenly in bottom of a greased 12x8-inch baking dish. Pour meat mixture over mush. Arrange cheese cubes over meat mixture.
4. Bake, uncovered, at 350°F 20 minutes, or until casserole is bubbly.

6 servings

Szededine Goulash

2 **pounds beef stew meat, cut in 1-inch pieces**
¼ **cup vegetable oil**
2 **cups sliced onion**
1 **garlic clove, minced**
1 **teaspoon salt**
1 **can (10 ounces) tomato purée,**
1 **cup water**
1 **cup dairy sour cream**
2 **teaspoons paprika**
2 **teaspoons caraway seed**
1 **can (16 ounces) sauerkraut, rinsed and drained**
2 **tablespoons snipped parsley**

1. Brown beef in oil in a skillet. Add onion and garlic. Sauté about 5 minutes; drain off excess fat.
2. Add salt, tomato purée, and water. Put into a 2½-quart casserole.
3. Bake, covered, at 325°F 2 hours, or until meat is tender, stirring occasionally. Remove cover. Stir in sour cream, paprika, caraway seed, and sauerkraut. Bake an additional 15 minutes, or until heated through. Sprinkle with parsley.

8 servings

Oven Beef Bake

2 pounds beef stew meat, cut in
    1-inch cubes
1 can (10¾ ounces) condensed cream
    of mushroom soup
1 can (10½ ounces) condensed onion
    soup
¼ cup dry vermouth

1. Put meat into a 2-quart casserole.
2. Combine mushroom soup, onion soup, and vermouth. Pour over meat.
3. Bake, covered, at 325°F 3 hours, or until meat is tender. Serve with **hot, cooked noodles.**

8 servings

Beef Bourguignon

¼ cup flour
1 teaspoon salt
½ teaspoon freshly ground black
    pepper
2 pounds beef stew meat, cut in
    2-inch cubes
¼ cup butter or margarine
1 medium onion, chopped
2 medium carrots, chopped
1 garlic clove, minced
2 cups dry red wine
1 can (6 ounces) mushroom crowns,
    drained, reserving liquid
1 bay leaf
3 tablespoons snipped parsley
½ teaspoon thyme
1 can (16 ounces) onions, drained

1. Combine flour, salt, and pepper; coat beef cubes.
2. Brown beef in butter in a skillet. Put into a 2-quart casserole.
3. Add onion, carrots, and garlic to skillet. Cook until tender but not brown. Add wine, liquid from mushrooms, bay leaf, parsley, and thyme. Pour over meat.
4. Bake, covered, at 350°F 2½ hours. Remove cover. Add onions and mushroom crowns. Bake an additional 30 minutes, or until meat is tender.

8 servings

Swiss Steak Mozzarella

2 pounds beef round steak, ½ inch
    thick
3 tablespoons flour
½ cup butter or margarine
1 can (16 ounces) tomatoes, cut up
1¼ teaspoons salt
¼ teaspoon basil
½ cup chopped green pepper
1½ cups (6 ounces) mozzarella cheese

1. Cut meat into serving-size pieces; coat with flour.
2. Melt butter in a skillet. Brown meat slowly on both sides. Put into a 12x8-inch baking dish.
3. Combine tomatoes, salt, basil, and green pepper. Pour over meat.
4. Bake, covered, at 350°F 1 hour, or until meat is tender. Remove cover. Sprinkle with cheese and bake an additional 5 minutes, or until cheese is melted.

8 servings

Stew with Cornbread Topping

1½ pounds beef stew meat, cut in
    ¾-inch cubes
  2 tablespoons butter or margarine
  2 medium onions, sliced
  1 garlic clove, minced
2¼ cups water
  1 can (8 ounces) tomato sauce
  ¼ bay leaf
  2 teaspoons salt
  ¼ teaspoon pepper
  4 carrots, cut in 1-inch pieces
  4 celery stalks, cut in 1-inch pieces
  ½ cup all-purpose flour
  2 teaspoons baking powder
  1 tablespoon sugar
  1 teaspoon salt
  1 cup cornmeal
  1 egg, beaten
  1 cup milk
  2 tablespoons vegetable oil
  1 tablespoon snipped parsley

1. Brown meat in butter in a skillet. Add onion and garlic, cooking until lightly brown. Stir in water, tomato sauce, bay leaf, 2 teaspoons salt, and the pepper. Put into a 2½-quart casserole.
2. Bake, covered, at 350°F 45 minutes. Remove bay leaf. Add carrots and celery. Bake, covered, an additional 25 minutes, or until meat and vegetables are tender.
3. Sift together flour, baking powder, sugar, and 1 teaspoon salt into a bowl. Mix in cornmeal. Add egg, milk, and oil. (Mix only until dry ingredients are moistened.)
4. Remove stew from oven. Pour topping over hot stew. Sprinkle with parsley.
5. Bake, uncovered, at 400°F 20 minutes, or until cornbread is golden brown.

6 servings

Slow Oven Beef Stew

  2 pounds beef stew meat, cut in
    1½-inch cubes
  2 medium onions, each cut in eighths
  3 celery stalks, cut in 1-inch
    diagonally sliced pieces
  4 medium carrots, pared and cut in
    half crosswise and lengthwise
  3 cups tomato juice
  ⅓ cup quick-cooking tapioca
  1 tablespoon sugar
  2 teaspoons salt
  ¼ teaspoon pepper
  1 bay leaf
  2 medium potatoes, pared and cut in
    ¼-inch-thick slices

1. Put all ingredients, except potatoes, into a 3-quart casserole.
2. Bake, covered, at 300°F 2½ hours. Remove bay leaf and stir in potatoes. Bake, covered, an additional 1 hour, or until meat and vegetables are tender.

8 servings

Cornbread Tamale Pie

1 pound ground beef
½ cup chopped onion
⅓ cup chopped celery
1 can (16 ounces) tomatoes (undrained)
1 can (12 ounces) whole kernel corn, drained
1 can (8 ounces) tomato sauce
1 tablespoon chili powder
1 teaspoon salt
¼ teaspoon pepper
¼ cup all-purpose flour
1½ teaspoons baking powder
½ teaspoon salt
¾ cup cornmeal
1 egg, beaten
½ cup milk
2 tablespoons vegetable oil

1. Brown ground beef, onion, and celery in a skillet; drain off excess fat. Add tomatoes, corn, tomato sauce, chili powder, 1 teaspoon salt, and the pepper; simmer 10 minutes.
2. Sift together flour, baking powder, and ½ teaspoon salt into a bowl. Mix in cornmeal. Stir in egg, milk, and oil. (Mix only until dry ingredients are moistened.)
3. Spoon hot meat mixture into a 2-quart casserole. Top with cornbread topping.
4. Bake, uncovered, at 425°F 15 minutes, or until topping is golden brown.

6 servings

Beef 'n' Peppers

1 garlic clove, minced
1½ pounds lean beef, cut in 1-inch cubes
2 tablespoons shortening
1 cup sliced fresh mushrooms
2 cans (10½ ounces each) brown gravy with onions
1 green pepper, cut in strips

1. Sauté garlic and beef in hot shortening in a skillet. Put into a 1½-quart casserole.
2. Combine mushrooms and gravy in skillet with drippings. Pour over meat.
3. Bake, covered, at 350°F 2 hours, or until meat is tender. Remove cover. Add pepper strips. Bake an additional 15 minutes, or until pepper is tender but still crisp. Serve over **hot, cooked rice** or **noodles.**

6 servings

Yankee Steak

2 pounds beef round steak, ½ inch thick
½ cup flour
2 teaspoons salt
½ teaspoon pepper
3 tablespoons vegetable oil
2 medium onions, thinly sliced
1 can (15 ounces) tomato sauce
⅛ teaspoon garlic powder

1. Cut meat into serving-size pieces. Combine flour, salt, and pepper; pound into steak.
2. Heat oil in a skillet. Brown meat slowly on both sides. Place in a 13x9-inch baking dish. Top with onion slices.
3. Combine tomato sauce and garlic powder. Pour over meat.
4. Bake, covered, at 350°F 1 hour, or until meat is tender.

8 servings

Creamy Baked Steak

1 **pound beef round tip steak**
4 **tablespoons flour**
½ **teaspoon salt**
2 **tablespoons vegetable oil**
1 **small onion, sliced**
1 **garlic clove, minced**
1 **can (10½ ounces) condensed beef broth**
1 **cup dairy sour cream**
2 **tablespoons sherry**
1 **can (3 ounces) sliced mushrooms, drained**

1. Cut steak into serving-size pieces. Sprinkle with 1 tablespoon flour and the salt.
2. Brown meat in oil in a skillet. Add onion and garlic.
3. Combine beef broth with remaining 3 tablespoons flour. Stir into skillet. Cook, stirring constantly, until mixture thickens. Put meat and sauce into a 12x8-inch baking dish.
4. Bake, covered, at 350°F 30 minutes, or until steak is tender. Remove cover. Combine sour cream, sherry, and mushrooms. Stir into meat mixture in baking dish. Bake an additional 5 minutes, or until heated through.

3 or 4 servings

Island-Style Short Ribs

4 **pounds lean beef short ribs**
½ **cup soy sauce**
⅓ **cup sugar**
2 **tablespoons vinegar**
1 **tablespoon vegetable oil**
1 **teaspoon ginger**
½ **teaspoon lemon pepper seasoning**
¼ **teaspoon garlic salt**
1 **large onion, finely chopped**
¼ **cup butter or margarine**
2 **cups water**

1. Cut meat from bones; reserve the bones. Trim off as much fat as possible. Cut meat into cubes. Put meat into a bowl.
2. Combine soy sauce, sugar, vinegar, oil, ginger, lemon pepper seasoning, and garlic salt. Pour over meat. Cover and refrigerate several hours or overnight.
3. Sauté onion in butter in a skillet. Remove onion; set aside.
4. Cook meat in skillet about 10 minutes. Add onion, marinade, and water. Put into a 2-quart casserole. Top with bones.
5. Bake, covered, at 325°F 1½ hours. Remove bones and bake, uncovered, an additional 30 minutes, or until meat is tender. To serve, spoon broth over **hot, cooked rice.**

8 servings

Veal Parmigiano

1 pound veal steak or cutlet, thinly
    sliced
1 teaspoon salt
⅛ teaspoon pepper
1 egg
2 cups plus 2 teaspoons water
⅓ cup grated Parmesan cheese
⅓ cup fine dry bread crumbs
¼ cup shortening
1 medium onion, finely chopped
1 can (6 ounces) tomato paste
1 teaspoon salt
½ teaspoon basil
6 slices mozzarella cheese

1. Cut veal into 8 pieces; sprinkle with 1 teaspoon salt and the pepper.
2. Lightly beat together egg and 2 teaspoons water.
3. Combine Parmesan cheese and bread crumbs.
4. Dip veal in egg wash, then Parmesan mixture. Refrigerate at least ½ hour.
5. Brown veal on both sides in shortening in a skillet. Remove to a 1½-quart shallow baking dish.
6. Sauté onion in skillet. Stir in tomato paste, 1 teaspoon salt, and basil. Simmer 5 minutes. Pour three fourths of the sauce over veal. Top with mozzarella cheese. Pour remaining sauce over cheese.
7. Bake, uncovered, at 350°F 20 to 25 minutes, or until mixture is bubbly.

4 servings

Northwoods Pork Chops

1 package (2¾ ounces) instant wild
    rice
¼ cup chopped celery
¼ cup chopped green pepper
¼ cup chopped onion
6 tablespoons butter or margarine
4 pork chops, ¾ inch thick
¼ cup flour
2 cups milk
½ teaspoon salt
⅛ teaspoon pepper
½ cup (2 ounces) shredded American
    cheese

1. Prepare wild rice according to package directions.
2. Sauté celery, green pepper, and onion in 4 tablespoons butter in a skillet. Combine with wild rice. Put into a 1½-quart shallow baking dish.
3. Brown pork chops on both sides in skillet. Place on top of wild rice mixture.
4. Melt remaining 2 tablespoons butter in skillet. Blend in flour. Gradually add milk, stirring until thickened and smooth. Add salt and pepper. Pour over pork chops.
5. Bake, covered, at 350°F 1 hour, or until chops are done. Sprinkle with cheese.

4 servings

Golden Pork Chop Bake

6 pork chops, 1 inch thick
2 tablespoons shortening
½ cup sliced celery
1 garlic clove, minced
2 cans (10¾ ounces each) condensed
    golden mushroom soup
1⅓ cups water
1⅓ cups packaged precooked rice
½ cup chopped tomato

1. Brown pork chops on both sides in shortening in a skillet. Remove chops from skillet; drain off excess fat.
2. Sauté celery and garlic in skillet. Combine with remaining ingredients. Spoon into a 2-quart shallow baking dish.
3. Arrange chops on top of rice mixture.
4. Bake, covered, at 350°F 1 hour, or until chops are tender.

6 servings

Baked Stuffed Pork Chops

4 rib pork chops, 1 inch thick
1 tablespoon finely chopped onion
¼ cup diced celery
2 tablespoons butter or margarine
1 cup soft bread crumbs
½ teaspoon salt
⅛ teaspoon poultry seasoning
2 tablespoons shortening
1 can (10¾ ounces) condensed cream
    of mushroom soup
⅓ cup water

1. Trim excess fat from pork chops. Slit each chop from bone side almost to fat, making a pocket.
2. Sauté onion and celery in butter in a skillet. Combine with bread crumbs, salt, and poultry seasoning. Stuff into pockets in chops.
3. Brown chops in shortening in skillet. Place in a 10x8-inch baking dish.
4. Add soup and water to drippings in skillet. Stir to dissolve brown particles. Pour over chops.
5. Bake, covered, at 350°F 1 hour, or until chops are tender.

4 servings

He-Man Casserole

½ cup chopped green onion
½ cup chopped green pepper
½ cup chopped celery
6 tablespoons butter or margarine
6 tablespoons flour
    Dash pepper
1 cup chicken broth
1½ cups milk
4 cups cubed cooked ham
1 package (10 ounces) frozen peas,
    thawed
4 cups hot, cooked mashed potatoes
    (stiff)
1 egg, beaten
1 cup (4 ounces) shredded Cheddar
    cheese

1. Sauté onion, green pepper, and celery in butter in a saucepan. Stir in flour and pepper. Gradually add broth and milk, stirring until thickened and smooth.
2. Mix with ham and peas. Put into a 3-quart casserole.
3. Combine potatoes, egg, and cheese. Spoon around edge of casserole mixture.
4. Bake, uncovered, at 375°F 45 minutes, or until mixture is bubbly.

8 servings

Calico Ham Bake

1 pound cooked ham
1 package (10 ounces) sharp Cheddar cheese
1 medium green pepper, chopped
4 eggs, beaten
2 cups milk

1. Grind ham and cheese together. Combine with green pepper, eggs, and milk. Put into a greased 8-inch square baking dish.
2. Bake, uncovered, at 325°F 1 hour, or until browned. Cut into squares to serve.

6 servings

Wild Rice-Ham Rolls

1½ cups uncooked wild rice
½ cup sliced green onion
¼ cup snipped parsley
¼ pound fresh mushrooms, sliced
¼ cup butter or margarine
¼ cup flour
½ teaspoon salt
¼ teaspoon pepper
¼ teaspoon nutmeg
½ cup dry white wine
2 cups milk
8 slices cooked ham, about ¼ inch thick

1. Prepare wild rice according to package directions. Add ¼ cup green onion and the parsley.
2. Sauté remaining ¼ cup green onion and mushrooms in butter in a skillet. Stir in flour, salt, pepper, and nutmeg. Gradually add wine, then milk, stirring until thickened and smooth.
3. Combine 1 cup sauce with 2 cups wild rice. Divide evenly on top of each ham slice. Spoon remaining rice on bottom of a lightly greased 12x9-inch shallow baking dish.
4. Roll up ham rolls to enclose filling. Place seam side down on rice in casserole. Spoon remaining sauce over ham rolls.
5. Bake, uncovered, at 350°F 20 minutes, or until heated through.

8 servings

Ham and Cheese Casserole Bread

⅔ cup chopped onion
3 tablespoons vegetable oil
2 cups all-purpose biscuit mix
1 cup chopped cooked ham
2 eggs
⅔ cup milk
1 teaspoon prepared mustard
1½ cups (6 ounces) shredded Cheddar cheese
2 tablespoons sesame seed
2 tablespoons snipped parsley
3 tablespoons butter or margarine, melted

1. Sauté onion in 1 tablespoon oil in a skillet.
2. Combine biscuit mix and ham.
3. Blend the remaining 2 tablespoons oil, eggs, milk, mustard, onion, and ¾ cup cheese. Stir into ham mixture. Spoon into a greased 1½-quart round casserole. Sprinkle with remaining ¾ cup cheese, sesame seed, parsley, and butter.
4. Bake, uncovered, at 350°F minutes, or until done. Cut into wedges to serve.

6 servings

Calico Supper Pie

1 can (10 biscuits) refrigerator biscuits
2 cups diced cooked ham
1 large tomato, sliced
¼ cup chopped green onion
1 cup (4 ounces) shredded Cheddar cheese
2 eggs, separated
½ cup milk
2 tablespoons flour
¼ cup (1 ounce) grated Parmesan cheese
1 tablespoon snipped parsley

1. Separate dough into biscuits. Place in a 9-inch deep pie pan; press over bottom and up sides to form crust. Sprinkle with ham. Top with tomato, green onion, and Cheddar cheese.
2. Beat egg yolks. Stir in milk and flour. Pour over cheese.
3. Beat egg whites until soft peaks form. Fold in Parmesan cheese and parsley. Spread over pie. Cover edge of crust with foil.
4. Bake at 350°F 25 minutes. Remove foil. Bake an additional 10 minutes, or until crust is golden brown. Let stand a few minutes before serving.

6 servings

Ham Wrap-Arounds

8 slices cooked ham, about ¼ inch thick
2 packages (10 ounces each) frozen broccoli spears, cooked and drained
3 cups cubed French bread, toasted*
1½ cups dry white wine
3 cups (12 ounces) shredded Swiss cheese
3 tablespoons flour
2 teaspoons prepared mustard
⅛ teaspoon garlic powder

1. Wrap ham slices around broccoli spears. Place in a 12x8-inch shallow baking dish. Sprinkle with bread cubes.
2. Heat wine in a saucepan. Mix cheese and flour. Gradually add to wine while stirring until smooth. Stir in mustard and garlic powder. Pour sauce over all in dish.
3. Bake, uncovered, at 350°F 30 minutes, or until heated through.

8 servings

* To toast cubed French bread, place on a baking sheet and put into a 350°F oven about 10 minutes.

Saucy Stuffed Peppers

6 medium green peppers
1½ pounds pork sausage meat
1 cup quick or old-fashioned oats, uncooked
⅔ cup tomato juice
1 can (10¾ ounces) condensed tomato soup
¼ cup milk
1 teaspoon Worcestershire sauce
⅛ teaspoon oregano

1. Cut ¼-inch slice from the top of each green pepper; remove seeds. Cook green peppers in **boiling water** about 5 minutes; drain.
2. Brown sausage in a skillet until lightly browned; drain off excess fat. Combine meat, oats, and tomato juice.
3. Fill green peppers with meat mixture. Stand upright in a 1½-quart shallow baking dish; add a small amount of **water.**
4. Bake, uncovered, at 350°F 45 to 50 minutes, or until done.
5. Serve with sauce made by heating together the soup, milk, Worcestershire sauce, and oregano.

6 servings

Ham and Asparagus Casserole

3 tablespoons butter or margarine
3 tablespoons flour
½ teaspoon dry mustard
1½ cups milk
1½ cups (6 ounces) shredded Cheddar cheese
2 cups cubed cooked ham
1 package (10 ounces) frozen cut-up asparagus, cooked and drained
⅛ teaspoon onion powder
Dash Tabasco
½ cup toasted slivered almonds

1. Melt butter in a saucepan. Stir in flour and mustard. Gradually add milk, stirring until thickened and smooth. Add cheese, stirring until smooth.
2. Combine with ham, asparagus, onion powder, and Tabasco. Put into a 1½-quart casserole. Sprinkle with almonds.
3. Bake, uncovered, at 350°F 20 minutes, or until heated through.

4 servings

Sausage-Green Bean Casserole

3 cups hot, cooked mashed potatoes
1 pound pork sausage links, cooked and drained
1 cup (4 ounces) shredded American cheese
1 package (9 ounces) frozen cut green beans, cooked and drained
1 can (8 ounces) small whole onions, drained
1 tablespoon chopped pimento

1. Layer half of the mashed potatoes, half of the sausage, and half of the cheese in a 1½-quart casserole.
2. Combine green beans, onions, and pimento. Spoon over cheese. Top with remaining potatoes, sausage, and cheese.
3. Bake, covered, at 350°F 30 minutes, or until heated through.

6 servings

Super Sausage Supper

1 **cup chopped onion**
1 **garlic clove, minced**
3 **carrots, pared and thinly sliced**
2 **tablespoons shortening**
1 **jar (32 ounces) sauerkraut, drained**
2 **cups apple cider**
½ **cup dry white wine**
¼ **teaspoon pepper**
3 **parsley sprigs**
1 **bay leaf**
1 **package (12 ounces) pork sausage links, cooked and drained**
1 **package (5 ounces) tiny smoked sausage links**
2 **links (8 ounces each) Polish sausage, cooked and drained**
2 **cans (16 ounces each) small white potatoes, drained**
1 **apple, cored and cut in chunks**

1. Sauté onion, garlic, and carrot in shortening in a skillet. Add sauerkraut, apple cider, wine, pepper, parsley, and bay leaf. Bring to a boil; reduce heat and simmer 15 minutes.
2. Stir in remaining ingredients. Remove bay leaf. Put into a 3-quart casserole.
3. Bake, covered, at 350°F 1 hour.

8 servings

Hearty Sausage Supper

1 **jar (16 ounces) applesauce**
1 **can (14 ounces) sauerkraut, drained**
⅓ **cup dry white wine**
2 **tablespoons firmly packed brown sugar**
1 **can (16 ounces) small white potatoes, drained**
1 **can (16 ounces) small whole onions, drained**
1 **ring (12 ounces) Polish sausage, slashed several times**
1 **tablespoon snipped parsley**

1. Mix applesauce, sauerkraut, wine, and brown sugar. Put into a 2½-quart casserole.
2. Arrange potatoes and onions around edge of casserole. Place sausage in center.
3. Bake, covered, at 350°F 45 to 50 minutes, or until heated through. Sprinkle with parsley.

4 servings

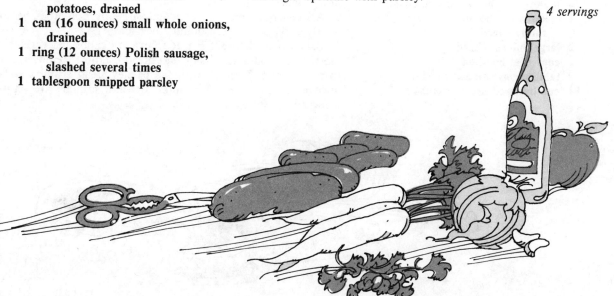

Smoked Sausage Dinner

1 medium onion, chopped
½ cup chopped green pepper
2 tablespoons butter or margarine
1 pound smoked sausage, cut in
  ½-inch pieces
1 can (16 ounces) tomatoes, cut up
1 cup uncooked noodles

1. Sauté onion and green pepper in butter in a skillet. Add sausage and brown lightly; drain off excess fat.
2. Stir in remaining ingredients. Put into a 1½-quart casserole.
3. Bake, covered, at 375°F 45 minutes, or until noodles are tender, stirring once.

4 servings

Lamb Curry

1½ pounds boneless lamb shoulder, cut
  in ¾-inch cubes
2 tablespoons shortening
1 teaspoon salt
1 teaspoon paprika
¼ teaspoon pepper
1 large onion, sliced
1 cup sliced celery
2¼ cups water
1 teaspoon curry powder
¼ cup flour
1 cup uncooked white rice

1. Brown lamb in shortening in a large saucepan. Sprinkle with salt, paprika, and pepper. Add onion, celery, and 2 cups water. Cover and simmer 1 hour, or until tender.
2. Combine curry powder, flour, and remaining ¼ cup water. Gradually add to saucepan, stirring until thickened and smooth.
3. Meanwhile, prepare rice according to package directions. Press rice in bottom and up sides of a 2-quart casserole. Pour lamb mixture into rice shell.
4. Bake, covered, at 350°F 20 minutes, or until casserole is bubbly. Serve with **chopped peanuts, shredded coconut,** and **chutney.**

6 servings

Smothered Lamb Chops

6 lamb rib chops
2 tablespoons butter or margarine
4 medium red potatoes, pared and
  thinly sliced
2 large onions, sliced
1½ cups beef bouillon
2 tablespoons snipped parsley
¼ cup buttered bread crumbs

1. Brown lamb chops on both sides in butter in a skillet. Place in a 2-quart shallow baking dish.
2. Arrange potatoes over chops and onions over potatoes. Season lightly with **salt.** Pour bouillon over all.
3. Bake, covered, at 375°F 1 hour, or until chops and vegetables are tender. Combine parsley and bread crumbs. Remove cover from casserole. Sprinkle with the parsley-bread crumbs. Bake, uncovered, at 450°F 10 minutes, or until crumbs are lightly browned.

6 servings

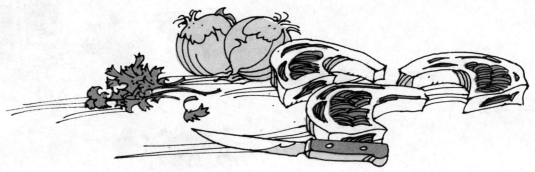

Franks and Scalloped Potatoes

6 medium potatoes, pared and thinly sliced
3 tablespoons finely chopped chives
3 tablespoons flour
1 teaspoon salt
¼ teaspoon pepper
3 tablespoons butter or margarine
2½ cups milk, heated
6 frankfurters, cut in pieces

1. Place one third of the potatoes in a greased 2½-quart casserole. Sprinkle with one third of the chives, one third of the flour, one third of the salt, and one third of the pepper. Dot with 1 tablespoon butter. Repeat twice. Pour milk over all.
2. Bake, covered, at 350°F 30 minutes. Remove cover. Stir in frankfurters. Bake, uncovered, an additional 50 minutes, or until potatoes are tender.

6 servings

Hot Dogs in Cornbread

1 package (8½ ounces) corn muffin mix
1 egg
⅓ cup milk
1 tablespoon instant minced onion
4 frankfurters, split in half lengthwise
1 teaspoon oregano
1 cup (4 ounces) shredded Cheddar cheese

1. Prepare corn muffin mix, using egg and milk, according to package directions. Stir onion into batter. Spread into a greased 1½-quart shallow baking dish.
2. Arrange frankfurters over batter. Sprinkle with oregano.
3. Bake, uncovered, at 400°F 15 minutes, or until golden brown. Sprinkle with cheese. Bake an additional 3 minutes, or until cheese is melted. Serve with **prepared mustard.**

4 servings

Macaroni and Cheese with Franks

1 package (8 ounces) elbow macaroni, cooked and drained
2 cups (8 ounces) shredded Cheddar cheese
1 can (13 ounces) evaporated milk
1 small onion, finely chopped
⅛ teaspoon pepper
1 package (16 ounces) frankfurters, cut in 1-inch pieces

1. Combine all ingredients. Put into a 2½-quart casserole.
2. Bake, covered, at 350°F 30 minutes, or until heated through, stirring occasionally.

6 servings

Dried Beef 'n' Noodles

1 cup diced celery
1 cup chopped onion
½ cup chopped green pepper
¼ cup shortening
2 tablespoons flour
2 cups milk
1 tablespoon Worcestershire sauce
  Dash Tabasco
½ cup (2 ounces) shredded American
    cheese
1 package (3 ounces) dried smoked
    beef, cut in pieces
2 cups cooked wide noodles
2 hard-cooked eggs, sliced

1. Sauté celery, onion, and green pepper in shortening in a skillet.
2. Stir in flour. Gradually add milk, stirring until thickened and smooth. Add Worcestershire sauce, Tabasco, and cheese, stirring until smooth. Stir in beef and noodles.
3. Put into a 1½-quart casserole. Top with hard-cooked egg slices.
4. Bake, covered, at 350°F 30 minutes, or until heated through.

4 servings

Corned Beef Casserole

½ cup chopped onion
¼ cup chopped green pepper
2 tablespoons shortening
1 can (12 ounces) corned beef, cut up
¾ cup water
1½ cups ketchup
1 package (10 ounces) frozen peas,
    thawed
1½ cups (about 6 ounces) shell
    macaroni, cooked and drained

1. Sauté onion and green pepper in shortening in a skillet. Stir in remaining ingredients. Put into a 2-quart casserole.
2. Bake, covered, at 350°F 30 minutes, or until heated through.

6 servings

Hearty Sandwich Squares

2 cups pancake mix
1 can (11 ounces) condensed Cheddar
    cheese soup
1 teaspoon prepared mustard
1¼ cups milk
8 slices (1 ounce each) luncheon meat
4 slices (1 ounce each) American
    cheese
¼ cup chopped onion
¼ cup chopped green pepper

1. Combine pancake mix, ¼ cup soup, mustard, and 1 cup milk.
2. Spread half the batter in a greased 8-inch square baking dish. Top with meat, cheese, onion, and green pepper. Spoon remaining batter over all.
3. Bake, uncovered, at 400°F 25 to 30 minutes, or until done. Cut into squares to serve. Heat together remaining soup and ¼ cup milk. Spoon over squares. Sprinkle with **snipped parsley.**

4 servings

Lamb Curry, 30

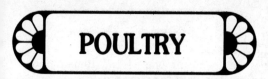

POULTRY

Poultry is popular all over the world, and what better way to serve it than in a casserole? Chicken can be mixed with fruit, rice, noodles, vegetables, and many other food combinations. And the result is a chicken casserole that will have everyone asking for the recipe. Looking for a way to use those leftovers? You'll find flavorful ideas here, such as Turkey Pot Pie or Chicken Bake.

Chicken Easy Oriental Style

¼ cup flour
1 teaspoon salt
¼ teaspoon pepper
4 chicken breasts, split in halves
¼ cup shortening
1 can (10¾ ounces) condensed cream of chicken soup
¼ cup dry white wine
¼ cup milk
1 can (4 ounces) water chestnuts, drained and sliced
¼ teaspoon ground ginger

1. Combine flour, salt, and pepper; coat chicken with mixture.
2. Brown chicken in shortening in skillet. Place in a 13x9-inch baking dish.
3. Combine soup, wine, milk, chestnuts, and ginger. Pour over chicken.
4. Bake, covered, at 350°F 1 hour, or until chicken is tender. If desired, sprinkle with snipped parsley.

4 servings

Chicken and Tomato Casserole

1 broiler-fryer chicken (about 3 pounds), cut up
3 tablespoons shortening
½ cup chopped onion
¼ cup chopped green pepper
1 can (28 ounces) tomatoes (undrained)
1 can (8 ounces) tomato sauce
1 can (6 ounces) tomato paste
1 teaspoon salt
1 teaspoon oregano

1. Brown chicken in shortening in a skillet. Place in a 2-quart casserole.
2. Sauté onion and green pepper in fat in skillet. Stir in remaining ingredients and pour over chicken.
3. Bake, covered, at 350°F 1 hour, or until chicken is tender. Serve with **hot, cooked spaghetti.**

4 servings

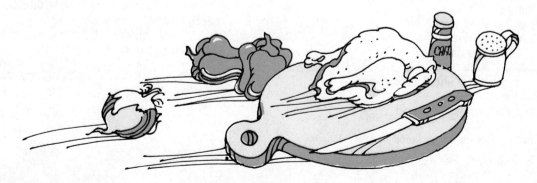

Chicken Novaes

2 jars (6 ounces each) tamales
1 can (4 ounces) sliced mushrooms, drained
2 cans (8 ounces each) tomato sauce
12 slices cooked chicken
2 cups cooked white rice
1 cup chopped green onion
2 cans (10¾ ounces each) condensed cream of chicken soup
1 cup (4 ounces) shredded Cheddar cheese
½ cup buttered bread crumbs

1. Remove paper from tamales. Cut in half crosswise and arrange in bottom of a 3-quart casserole.
2. Over the tamales, layer mushrooms, 1 can tomato sauce, chicken, rice, and onion. Top with the remaining can of tomato sauce. Spoon chicken soup over all, inserting a knife so soup will seep through.
3. Combine cheese and bread crumbs. Sprinkle over top of casserole mixture.
4. Bake, covered, at 350°F 30 minutes, or until bubbly.

12 servings

Swiss Chicken Bake

6 chicken breasts, split in halves, boned, and skin removed
1½ cups (6 ounces) shredded Swiss cheese
1 can (10¾ ounces) condensed cream of chicken soup
½ cup sherry
3 cups packaged herb stuffing mix
1 tablespoon butter or margarine

1. Place chicken breasts in a 13x9-inch baking dish. Sprinkle with cheese.
2. Combine soup and sherry; pour over Swiss cheese. Evenly spoon dressing over all. Dot with butter.
3. Bake, covered, at 350°F 1 hour, or until chicken is tender.

6 servings

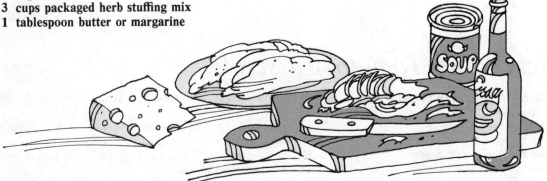

Thyme-Chicken Casserole

4 chicken breasts, split in halves
1 teaspoon salt
¼ teaspoon pepper
¼ cup butter or margarine
1 can (10¾ ounces) condensed cream of mushroom soup
¼ cup dry white wine
1 can (4 ounces) sliced mushrooms, drained
¼ cup chopped green pepper
¼ teaspoon thyme
1 tablespoon instant minced onion

1. Season chicken with salt and pepper. Brown in butter in a skillet. Arrange, skin side up, in a 13x9-inch baking dish.
2. Blend soup into drippings. Slowly stir in wine. Add remaining ingredients; heat thoroughly. Pour over chicken.
3. Bake, covered, at 350°F 50 minutes. Remove cover and bake an additional 10 minutes, or until chicken is tender.

4 servings

Italian Baked Chicken

¼ cup butter or margarine, melted
1 tablespoon lemon juice
1 broiler-fryer chicken (about 3 pounds), cut up
1 package (1½ ounces) spaghetti sauce mix
⅔ cup fine dry bread crumbs
½ to 1 cup half-and-half
1 cup (4 ounces) shredded mozzarella cheese

1. Combine butter and lemon juice. Dip chicken pieces in butter mixture.
2. Combine spaghetti sauce mix and bread crumbs; coat chicken pieces with mixture.
3. Place chicken pieces, skin side up, in a 1½-quart shallow baking dish. Pour half-and-half around and between chicken pieces.
4. Bake, covered, at 350°F 1 hour, or until chicken is tender. Top with cheese and bake 2 minutes, or until cheese is melted.

4 servings

Crispy Chicken with Curried Fruit

1 cup corn flake crumbs
½ teaspoon salt
Dash pepper
1 broiler-fryer chicken (about 3 pounds), cut up
½ cup evaporated milk
Curried Fruit

1. Combine crumbs, salt, and pepper. Dip chicken pieces in milk. Roll in crumb mixture. Place chicken pieces in a 1½-quart shallow baking dish.
2. Bake, uncovered, at 350°F with Curried Fruit 1 hour, or until chicken is tender.

4 servings

Curried Fruit

1 can (16 ounces) peach halves, drained*
1 can (8½ ounces) pineapple chunks, drained*
4 maraschino cherries
¼ cup butter or margarine, melted
½ cup firmly packed brown sugar
1 tablespoon curry powder

1. Put fruits into a 1½-quart casserole. Combine butter, brown sugar, and curry powder. Spoon over fruits.
2. Bake, covered, at 350°F 1 hour. Serve with **hot, cooked rice.**

4 servings

* The drained liquids can be refrigerated and used in gelatin salads.

Chicken and Rice

2 cups cooked white rice
½ cup milk
2 tablespoons chopped pimento
1 can (10¾ ounces) condensed cream of celery soup
1 can (10¾ ounces) condensed cream of mushroom soup
1 broiler-fryer chicken (about 3 pounds), cut up
1 package (1⅜ ounces) dry onion soup mix

1. Combine rice, milk, pimento, celery soup, and mushroom soup. Pour into a greased 13x9-inch baking dish.
2. Dip chicken pieces in **milk,** then roll in onion soup mix. Arrange chicken pieces over rice mixture.
3. Bake, covered, at 350°F 1 hour, or until chicken is tender.

4 servings

Chicken and Rice Valencia

1 broiler-fryer chicken (about 3 pounds), cut up
¼ cup olive oil
1 medium onion, finely chopped
1 medium green pepper, slivered
1 can (10 ounces) tomatoes (undrained)
1 bay leaf
¾ cup water
Dash ground saffron (optional)
1 cup drained stuffed olives
1 package (6 ounces) Spanish rice mix
½ cup chopped celery

1. Brown chicken pieces in olive oil in a skillet.
2. Add remaining ingredients, except rice and celery. Place in a 2-quart casserole.
3. Bake, covered, at 350°F 1 hour, or until chicken is tender.
4. Meanwhile, prepare rice according to package directions. Stir celery into rice. Spread on hot serving platter.
5. Remove bay leaf from chicken. Spoon chicken and sauce over rice.

4 servings

Chicken Surprise

½ cup chopped onion
1 tablespoon butter or margarine
1 tablespoon cornstarch
¾ cup orange juice
2 tablespoons prepared mustard
½ cup sherry
2 cups chopped cooked chicken
½ cup raisins
½ cup sliced celery

1. Sauté onion in butter in a skillet. Stir in cornstarch. Gradually add orange juice, then mustard and sherry, stirring until thickened and smooth.
2. Place chicken, raisins, and celery in a 1-quart casserole. Pour sauce over all; mix.
3. Bake, covered, at 325°F 30 minutes, or until heated through. Serve in **chow mein noodle** or **patty shells** and garnish with **orange twists.**

4 servings

Chicken Breasts with Sour Cream

8 chicken breasts, split in halves,
   boned, and skin removed
16 bacon slices
3 packages (3 ounces each) smoked
   sliced beef
1 can (10¾ ounces) condensed cream
   of mushroom soup
2 cups dairy sour cream

1. Roll each chicken breast in 1 bacon slice. (Another half bacon slice may be needed if the breast is a large one, so that all of it will be surrounded by the bacon.)
2. Shred beef and place in a 13x9-inch baking dish. Top with chicken breasts.
3. Combine soup and sour cream. Spoon over chicken breasts.
4. Bake, uncovered, at 275°F 3 hours, or until chicken is tender. Cover lightly with foil if it begins to get too brown.

8 servings

Chicken Pie

1¼ cups water
1 cup milk
1 package (⅞ ounce) chicken gravy
   mix
1 package (10 ounces) frozen peas,
   thawed
2 tablespoons chopped pimento
2 cups cubed cooked chicken
1 tablespoon finely chopped onion
1 teaspoon snipped parsley
2 cups all-purpose biscuit mix

1. Combine ¾ cup water, milk, and gravy mix in a saucepan; bring to a boil.
2. Stir in peas, pimento, and chicken; heat thoroughly.
3. Stir onion, parsley, and remaining ½ cup water into biscuit mix, stirring until thoroughly moistened.
4. Pour hot chicken mixture into an 11x7-inch shallow baking dish. Roll or pat out dough to fit top of baking dish. Set on chicken mixture.
5. Bake, uncovered, at 450°F 10 to 12 minutes, or until topping is golden brown.

6 servings

Chicken Mac

1 package (7¼ ounces) macaroni and
   cheese dinner
1 tablespoon instant minced onion
2 tablespoons chopped celery
2 tablespoons chopped green pepper
1 garlic clove, minced
2 tablespoons butter or margarine
1 can (8¾ ounces) whole kernel corn,
   drained
1 can (10¾ ounces) condensed cream
   of chicken soup
1½ cups chopped cooked chicken or
   turkey
2 tablespoons snipped parsley
⅓ cup buttered bread crumbs

1. Prepare dinner according to package directions, except use ½ cup milk.
2. Sauté onion, celery, green pepper, and garlic in butter in a skillet. Combine with corn, soup, chicken, and prepared dinner. Put into a greased 1½-quart casserole.
3. Combine parsley and bread crumbs. Sprinkle over top of casserole mixture.
4. Bake, covered, at 350°F 25 minutes, or until heated through.

4 servings

Chicken Artichoke Casserole

⅓ cup butter or margarine
¼ cup flour
1¾ cups milk
   Dash ground red pepper
1 garlic clove, minced
¼ cup (1 ounce) shredded Cheddar
   cheese
1½ ounces Gruyère cheese, cut up
2 cups chopped cooked chicken
1 can (4 ounces) button mushrooms,
   drained
1 can (14 ounces) artichoke hearts,
   drained

1. Melt butter in a saucepan. Stir in flour. Gradually add milk, stirring until thickened and smooth.
2. Add red pepper, garlic, and cheese, stirring until smooth. Blend in chicken, mushrooms, and artichoke hearts. Pour into a 2-quart casserole.
3. Bake, covered, at 350°F 30 minutes, or until heated through. Sprinkle with **paprika.**

6 servings

Chicken-Green Noodle Casserole

½ cup chopped onion
½ cup slivered almonds
1 cup sliced fresh mushrooms
¼ cup butter or margarine
3 cups cooked spinach (green) noodles
1 cup milk
2 cans (10¾ ounces each) condensed
   cream of chicken soup
3 cups chopped cooked chicken
¼ teaspoon pepper
⅓ cup buttered bread crumbs

1. Sauté onion, almonds, and mushrooms in butter in a skillet. Combine with remaining ingredients, except bread crumbs. Put into a 2½-quart casserole.
2. Bake, covered, at 350°F 30 minutes. Remove cover. Sprinkle with bread crumbs and bake an additional 15 minutes, or until heated through.

8 servings

Chicken-Chip Bake

2 cups chopped cooked chicken
2 cups sliced celery
1 can (8 ounces) pineapple chunks,
   drained
¾ cup mayonnaise
⅓ cup toasted slivered almonds
2 tablespoons lemon juice
2 teaspoons finely chopped onion
½ teaspoon salt
½ cup (2 ounces) shredded American
   cheese
1 cup crushed potato chips

1. Combine chicken, celery, pineapple, mayonnaise, almonds, lemon juice, onion, and salt. Put into a 1½-quart casserole. Sprinkle with cheese and potato chips.
2. Bake, uncovered, at 350°F 30 minutes, or until heated through.

4 to 6 servings

Chicken Bake

8 slices white bread, crusts removed
4 cups chopped cooked chicken or
   turkey
1 jar (4½ ounces) mushroom stems
   and pieces, drained
1 can (4 ounces) water chestnuts,
   drained and sliced
8 slices (1 ounce each) Cheddar
   cheese
¼ cup mayonnaise
4 eggs, well beaten
2 cups milk
1 teaspoon salt
2 cans (10¾ ounces each) condensed
   cream of mushroom soup
1 tablespoon chopped pimento
½ cup buttered bread crumbs

1. Place bread in a 13x9-inch baking dish. Top with chicken, mushrooms, water chestnuts, cheese, and mayonnaise.
2. Combine eggs, milk, and salt. Pour over all in casserole.
3. Mix soup and pimento; spread over top. Cover and refrigerate overnight.
4. Bake, covered, at 325°F 1 hour. Remove cover; sprinkle with bread crumbs and bake an additional 15 minutes, or until set. Let stand a few minutes before serving.

8 servings

Hens in Wine

1 tablespoon rosemary
1 cup dry white wine
⅓ cup flour
1 teaspoon salt
½ teaspoon pepper
1 teaspoon snipped parsley
4 Rock Cornish hens, quartered
½ cup butter or margarine
1 pound small fresh mushrooms

1. Soak rosemary in wine 1 hour.
2. Combine flour, salt, pepper, and parsley. Coat hen quarters with flour mixture.
3. Brown hen quarters in butter in a skillet. Place in a 12x8-inch baking dish. Add wine mixture.
4. Bake, uncovered, at 350°F 30 minutes.
5. Meanwhile, sauté mushrooms in butter in skillet. Add to baking dish. Bake an additional 15 minutes, or until hen quarters are tender.

4 servings

Chicken à la King

½ cup sliced fresh mushrooms
¼ cup butter or margarine
¼ cup flour
2 cups milk
1 teaspoon salt
1½ cups cooked noodles
2 cups chopped cooked chicken or turkey
¾ cup (3 ounces) shredded Cheddar cheese
1 cup cooked peas
1 tablespoon instant minced onion
2 teaspoons Worcestershire sauce
1 tablespoon ketchup
Dash Tabasco

1. Sauté mushrooms in butter in a skillet. Stir in flour. Gradually add milk, stirring until thickened and smooth. Stir in remaining ingredients. Put into a 2-quart casserole.
2. Bake, covered, at 350°F 30 minutes, or until heated through.

4 servings

Chicken and Wild Rice

¾ cup uncooked wild rice
4 cups chopped cooked chicken
1 cup sherry
1 cup chicken broth
1 small onion, chopped
1 can (8 ounces) mushroom slices, drained
¼ cup butter or margarine, melted
1 can (10¾ ounces) condensed cream of mushroom soup
1 can (10¾ ounces) condensed cream of chicken soup
2 packages (10 ounces each) frozen broccoli or asparagus spears, cooked and drained
1 cup (4 ounces) shredded Cheddar cheese

1. Cook wild rice according to package directions.
2. Combine rice with remaining ingredients, except broccoli and cheese.
3. Spread half the rice mixture in a 13x9-inch baking dish. Top with broccoli. Evenly spread remaining rice mixture over all.
4. Bake, uncovered, at 350°F 45 minutes, or until heated through. Sprinkle with cheese and bake an additional 5 minutes, or until cheese is melted.

8 servings

Turkey Pot Pie

2 cups chopped cooked turkey
2 cans (10¾ ounces each) condensed
 cream of celery soup
½ cup milk
½ teaspoon Worcestershire sauce
 Dash pepper
6 cooked small onions
1 cup cooked cubed potato
1 cup cooked sliced carrot
⅓ cup shortening
1 cup self-rising flour
4 tablespoons cold water

1. Combine turkey, soup, milk, Worcestershire sauce, pepper, onions, potato, and carrot. Put into a 2-quart casserole.
2. Cut shortening into flour. Add water, a tablespoon at a time, mixing lightly until dough can be formed into a ball. (If necessary, add a little more water to make dough hold together.) Let rest 5 minutes.
3. Roll dough out on a lightly floured board or canvas to fit top of casserole. Cut slits to allow steam to escape. Adjust over filling; flute edges.
4. Bake, uncovered, at 425°F 20 minutes, or until pastry is golden brown.

6 servings

Turkey 'n' Dressing Bake

½ cup diced celery
¼ cup minced onion
3 tablespoons butter or margarine
3¼ cups quick chicken broth (dissolve 4
 chicken bouillon cubes in 3¼
 cups boiling water)
5 cups coarse whole wheat bread
 crumbs; reserve ½ cup crumbs
 for topping
¼ cup snipped parsley
½ teaspoon salt
¼ teaspoon pepper
1 egg, slightly beaten
2 tablespoons flour
2 eggs, beaten
¼ teaspoon crushed leaf sage
¼ teaspoon celery salt
⅛ teaspoon pepper
 Thin slices of cooked roast turkey
1 tablespoon butter or margarine,
 melted

1. Sauté celery and onion in 3 tablespoons hot butter in a large skillet about 5 minutes. Combine with 1¾ cups of the chicken broth, 4½ cups bread crumbs, parsley, salt, pepper, and slightly beaten egg; mix lightly with a fork. Spoon mixture over bottom of a shallow 2-quart baking dish; set aside.
2. Mix flour and ¼ cup cooled broth in a saucepan until smooth. Gradually add remaining broth, stirring constantly until thickened and smooth. Remove from heat. Add sauce gradually to eggs while beating. Blend in seasonings.
3. Arrange the desired amount of turkey over dressing in baking dish. Pour the sauce over all.
4. Toss reserved crumbs with melted butter; spoon over top.
5. Bake, uncovered, at 350°F 30 to 40 minutes, or until egg mixture is set. Garnish with **snipped parsley.**

6 servings

FISH and SEAFOOD

Our lakes and oceans are full of the many fish and seafoods we enjoy. Tuna, shrimp, lobster, oysters, sole, and many other varieties can be adapted to casseroles, and you'll be delighted with the results! If you're on a budget, let it be Tuna-Rice Pie, and if it's time to splurge, Seafood Creole will fill the order.

Tunaroni Casserole

¼ cup chopped onion
2 tablespoons snipped parsley
2 tablespoons butter or margarine
2 tablespoons flour
½ teaspoon salt
⅛ teaspoon pepper
2 cups milk
2 cups cooked elbow macaroni
1 can (28 ounces) tomatoes, drained and cut up
2 cans (6½ or 7 ounces each) tuna, drained and flaked
¼ cup buttered bread crumbs

1. Sauté onion and parsley in butter in a skillet. Stir in flour, salt, and pepper. Gradually add milk, stirring until thickened and smooth.
2. Stir in macaroni, tomatoes, and tuna. Put into a 2-quart casserole. Sprinkle with bread crumbs.
3. Bake, covered, at 375°F 30 minutes, or until mixture is bubbly.

6 servings

Tuna for Two

1 can (2 ounces) sliced mushrooms, drained
¼ cup sliced green onion
¼ teaspoon dill weed
2 tablespoons butter or margarine
1 tablespoon lemon juice or wine
1 can (7½ ounces) semicondensed cream of mushroom soup with wine
1 can (6½ or 7 ounces) tuna, drained and flaked
1 tablespoon chopped pimento
1 package (10 ounces) frozen broccoli spears, cooked and drained
2 tablespoons grated Parmesan cheese

1. Sauté mushrooms, onion, and dill weed in butter in a saucepan. Stir in lemon juice, soup, tuna, and pimento.
2. Arrange broccoli spears in 2 or 3 individual casseroles. Spoon tuna mixture over broccoli. Sprinkle with Parmesan cheese.
3. Bake, uncovered, at 350°F 20 minutes, or until heated through.

2 or 3 servings

Tuna-Idaho Casserole

¼ cup finely chopped onion
½ cup chopped celery
3 tablespoons butter or margarine
3 tablespoons flour
1¾ cups milk
1 tablespoon lemon juice
1 teaspoon grated lemon peel
½ teaspoon salt
¼ teaspoon dill weed
Dash pepper
1 package (10 ounces) frozen peas,
cooked and drained
1 can (12 ounces) tuna, drained and
flaked
2 cups frozen Idaho potato puffs

1. Sauté onion and celery in butter in a saucepan. Stir in flour. Gradually add milk, stirring until thickened and smooth.
2. Add remaining ingredients, except potatoes. Spoon into a 1½-quart casserole. Top with potato puffs.
3. Bake, uncovered, at 450°F 20 minutes, or until puffs are golden brown and mixture is heated through.

4 servings

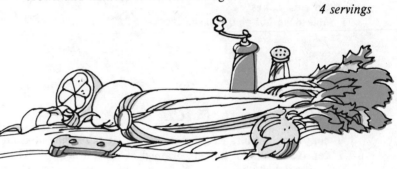

Confetti Casserole

1 can (10¾ ounces) condensed cream
of mushroom soup
1 can (16 ounces) peas (undrained)
2 tablespoons chopped pimento
¼ cup chopped celery
¼ cup chopped green pepper
1 tablespoon Worcestershire sauce
2 cans (6½ or 7 ounces each) tuna,
drained and flaked
1 cup (4 ounces) shredded American
cheese
1 can (3 ounces) French-fried onions

1. Combine soup, peas with ½ cup liquid, pimento, celery, green pepper, and Worcestershire sauce. Mix in tuna and cheese.
2. Put half the mixture into a 2-quart casserole. Sprinkle with half the onions; repeat.
3. Bake, uncovered, at 375°F 30 minutes, or until mixture is bubbly.

6 servings

Tuna-Rice Pie

2 cups cooked white rice
2 tablespoons butter or margarine,
melted
3 eggs, beaten
⅓ cup chopped pitted ripe olives
¾ cup milk
1 can (6½ or 7 ounces) tuna, drained
and flaked
3 green onions, sliced
Dash ground red pepper
1 cup (4 ounces) shredded Swiss
cheese

1. Combine rice, butter, 1 egg, and ripe olives. Spread evenly onto sides and bottom of a greased 9-inch pie plate.
2. Combine remaining 2 eggs, milk, tuna, onion, and red pepper. Pour into rice-lined pie plate. Sprinkle with cheese.
3. Bake, uncovered, at 350°F 15 minutes. Turn oven control to 300°F and bake an additional 10 minutes, or until set.

4 servings

Tuna Dinner

2 cups cooked green beans
1 can (10¾ ounces) condensed cream
   of chicken soup
1 cup mayonnaise
2 cans (7 ounces each) tuna packed in
   water (undrained)
½ cup corn flakes
1 tablespoon butter or margarine

1. Combine beans, soup, mayonnaise, and tuna. Put into a 1½-quart casserole. Top with corn flakes. Dot with butter.
2. Bake, uncovered, at 350°F 30 minutes, or until heated through.

6 servings

Salmon with Rice

1⅓ cups cooked white rice
1 can (15½ ounces) salmon, drained
   and flaked
1 large tomato, chopped
¼ cup chopped onion
1 tablespoon snipped parsley
½ cup whipping cream, whipped
½ teaspoon salt
   Dash ground red pepper
1 tablespoon lemon juice
½ cup (2 ounces) freshly grated
   Parmesan cheese

1. Combine all ingredients, except cheese. Put into a 1½-quart casserole. Sprinkle with cheese.
2. Bake, covered, at 350°F 20 minutes, or until bubbly.

4 servings

Individual Salmon-Green Bean Casseroles

1 package (9 ounces) frozen Italian
   green beans, cooked and drained
1 package (9 ounces) frozen artichoke
   hearts, cooked and drained
1 can (15½ ounces) salmon, drained
   and flaked
½ cup canned Hollandaise sauce
½ cup dairy sour cream
½ teaspoon grated lemon peel
¼ teaspoon crushed tarragon
⅛ teaspoon pepper
⅓ cup toasted slivered almonds

1. Combine beans, artichoke hearts, and salmon. Spoon into 6 individual casseroles.
2. Combine Hollandaise sauce, sour cream, lemon peel, tarragon, and pepper. Spoon evenly over salmon mixture. Sprinkle with almonds.
3. Bake, uncovered, at 350°F 20 minutes, or until heated through.

6 servings

Baked Salmon Squares

1 can (15½ ounces) salmon, drained and flaked
½ cup fine dry bread crumbs
1 can (10¾ ounces) condensed cream of celery soup
¼ cup dairy sour cream
2 eggs, beaten

1. Combine all ingredients. Put into a greased 8-inch square baking dish.
2. Bake, uncovered, at 325°F 1 hour, or until set. Cut into squares and serve with **creamed spinach.**

6 servings

Shrimp and Rice Supreme

1 medium onion, thinly sliced
⅓ cup chopped green pepper
½ cup sliced fresh mushrooms
¼ cup butter or margarine
¼ cup flour
½ teaspoon salt
Dash ground red pepper
2 cups milk
1 tablespoon Worcestershire sauce
2 cups cooked white rice
1 pound cooked and cleaned shrimp

1. Sauté onion, green pepper, and mushrooms in butter in a skillet. Stir in flour, salt, and red pepper. Gradually add milk, stirring until thickened and smooth.
2. Combine sauce with remaining ingredients. Put into a 2-quart casserole.
3. Bake, covered, at 350°F 30 minutes, or until bubbly.

6 servings

Shrimp Florentine

1 package (10 ounces) frozen spinach, cooked and squeezed
1 pound cooked and cleaned shrimp
1 can (10¾ ounces) condensed cream of chicken soup
¼ cup sherry
1 tablespoon snipped parsley
Dash pepper
½ cup (2 ounces) shredded Cheddar cheese
¼ cup buttered bread crumbs

1. Put spinach into a 1½-quart casserole.
2. Blend shrimp, soup, sherry, parsley, and pepper. Spoon over spinach.
3. Combine cheese and crumbs. Sprinkle over all.
4. Bake, covered, at 350°F 30 minutes, or until heated through.

4 servings

Shrimp Lasagne

½ cup chopped onion
1 garlic clove, minced
2 tablespoons butter or margarine
2 cans (8 ounces each) tomato sauce
1 can (6 ounces) tomato paste
½ cup water
1 tablespoon basil
2 teaspoons oregano
¼ teaspoon pepper
½ pound lasagne noodles
12 ounces cooked and cleaned shrimp
⅓ cup sliced pitted ripe olives
2 cups (8 ounces) shredded mozzarella cheese
1 carton (16 ounces) cream-style cottage cheese
½ cup (2 ounces) grated Parmesan cheese

1. Sauté onion and garlic in butter in a saucepan. Add tomato sauce, tomato paste, water, and seasonings. Simmer 25 minutes.
2. Meanwhile, cook noodles according to package directions.
3. Add shrimp and olives to sauce.
4. Layer half the noodles, half the mozzarella cheese, half the cottage cheese, and half the sauce in a 13x9-inch baking dish. Repeat layers. Sprinkle with Parmesan cheese.
5. Bake, covered, at 350°F 20 minutes. Remove cover and bake an additional 15 minutes, or until heated through. Let stand a few minutes before serving.

8 servings

Seafood Creole

1 medium onion, chopped
1 garlic clove, minced
½ cup chopped green pepper
½ cup sliced celery
3 tablespoons butter or margarine
1½ tablespoons flour
1 can (28 ounces) tomatoes (undrained)
1 bay leaf
1 teaspoon salt
1 teaspoon sugar
½ teaspoon allspice
1 tablespoon Worcestershire sauce
¼ teaspoon Tabasco
1 can (6½ or 7 ounces) tuna, drained and flaked
1 pound cooked and cleaned shrimp
1 can (7½ ounces) Alaska King crab, drained and flaked
2 tablespoons snipped parsley

1. Sauté onion, garlic, green pepper, and celery in butter in a skillet. Stir in flour. Add tomatoes, stirring until slightly thickened.
2. Combine with remaining ingredients, except parsley. Put into a 2-quart casserole.
3. Bake, covered, at 350°F 30 minutes, or until bubbly. Remove bay leaf. Sprinkle with parsley and serve over **hot, cooked rice.**

8 servings

Pimento-Crab Meat Strata Supreme

1 can (7½ ounces) Alaska King crab,
    drained and flaked
½ cup chopped celery
¼ cup chopped onion
¾ cup mayonnaise
    Dash ground red pepper
12 slices white bread, crusts removed
    Butter or margarine, softened
3 jars (4 ounces each) whole
    pimentos, each pimento cut in 2
    or 3 large pieces
4 cups (1 pound) shredded Swiss
    cheese
5 eggs
3 cups milk
1 teaspoon salt
⅛ teaspoon pepper
¼ teaspoon dry mustard

1. Mix crab, celery, and onion. Blend in mayonnaise and red pepper. Set aside.
2. Spread both sides of the bread slices with butter. Place half the bread slices in a layer in a 3-quart shallow baking dish.
3. Arrange half the pimento pieces, half the crab mixture, and one third the cheese over the bread. Repeat layering, using remainder of the crab mixture, pimento, and second third of the cheese. Cover with reserved bread slices and sprinkle with the remaining cheese.
4. Beat together remaining ingredients until frothy and blended. Pour over all. Let stand 1 hour.
5. Bake, uncovered, at 325°F 1 hour, or until puffed and brown. If desired, garnish with pimento strips, green pepper strips, and sprigs of parsley.

6 to 8 servings

Smoked Oyster and Corn Casserole

1 egg, beaten
½ cup evaporated milk
1 can (16 ounces) whole kernel corn,
    drained
1 tablespoon instant minced onion
1 teaspoon soy sauce
1 can (3½ ounces) smoked oysters,
    drained
¼ cup coarsely crushed soda crackers

1. Combine egg, evaporated milk, corn, onion, and soy sauce. Put into a 1-quart casserole.
2. Scatter oysters over top. Sprinkle with cracker crumbs.
3. Bake, uncovered, at 325°F 30 minutes, or until mixture is bubbly. Stir before serving.

4 servings

Savory Rice and Lobster

1 **large lobster tail (about 10 ounces)**
  Paprika
3 **tablespoons butter or margarine**
2 **teaspoons lemon juice**
¼ **teaspoon salt**
¼ **teaspoon garlic powder**
¼ **teaspoon onion powder**
¼ **teaspoon oregano**
  Dash pepper
2 **tablespoons dry white wine**
1 **package (6 ounces) long-grain and**
    wild rice, cooked according to
    package directions

1. Cook lobster in **boiling salted water** 5 minutes.
2. Rinse lobster tail with cold water. Remove meat from shell and cut up. Sprinkle lobster pieces with paprika.
3. Brown lobster lightly in butter in a skillet. Sprinkle with lemon juice. Combine with remaining ingredients. Put into a 1-quart casserole.
4. Bake, covered, at 325°F 25 minutes, or until heated through. If desired, sprinkle with snipped parsley.

4 servings

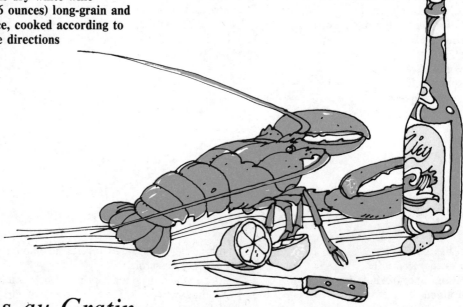

Scallops au Gratin

2 **tablespoons butter or margarine**
2 **tablespoons flour**
1 **cup milk**
1 **package (12 ounces) frozen scallops,**
    thawed and drained
1 **can (4 ounces) mushroom slices,**
    drained
¼ **cup chopped green onion**
1 **teaspoon grated lemon peel**
½ **teaspoon salt**
⅛ **teaspoon garlic powder**
½ **cup (4 ounces) shredded Cheddar**
    cheese
¼ **cup fine dry bread crumbs**
4 **English muffins, split and toasted**
8 **tomato slices**

1. Melt butter in a skillet. Stir in flour. Gradually add milk, stirring until thickened and smooth.
2. Stir in scallops, mushrooms, green onion, lemon peel, salt, and garlic powder. Put into a 1-quart casserole.
3. Mix cheese and bread crumbs. Sprinkle over all.
4. Bake, covered, at 325°F 25 minutes, or until mixture is bubbly. To serve, top each English muffin half with a tomato slice. Spoon scallop mixture over tomato.

4 servings

Crispy Chicken with Curried Fruit, 35

Fish and Vegetable Casserole

1½ pounds frozen fish steaks, thawed and cut in chunks
1 can (16 ounces) cut green beans, drained
1 can (16 ounces) sliced carrots, drained
¼ cup butter or margarine
¼ cup flour
1 teaspoon salt
½ teaspoon pepper
⅔ cup milk
1½ cups chicken broth
1 can (10¾ ounces) condensed tomato soup
½ teaspoon rosemary
3 cups hot, cooked mashed potatoes

1. Put fish, green beans, and carrots into a 2½-quart casserole.
2. Melt butter in a saucepan. Stir in flour, salt, and pepper. Gradually add milk and broth, stirring until thickened and smooth.
3. Stir in soup and rosemary. Pour over fish and vegetables.
4. Bake, covered, at 350°F 15 minutes. Remove cover and spoon potatoes around edge of casserole. Bake an additional 15 minutes, or until fish is flaky and mixture is heated through.

6 servings

Seafood Continental

6 sole fillets
¼ cup chopped celery
¼ cup chopped green pepper
⅛ teaspoon leaf tarragon
2 tablespoons butter or margarine
1⅓ cups water
1½ cups packaged precooked rice
½ pound cooked and cleaned shrimp, cut up
1 can (10¾ ounces) condensed cream of celery soup
⅓ cup dry white wine

1. Line the sides of 6 well-greased 6-ounce individual casseroles or custard cups with sole fillets.
2. Sauté celery, green pepper, and tarragon in butter in a saucepan. Add water; bring to a boil. Stir in rice. Cover and cook 5 minutes.
3. Stir in half the shrimp and ¼ cup soup. Spoon into fish-lined cups.
4. Bake, uncovered, at 350°F 30 minutes. Unmold onto a serving platter. Serve with sauce made by heating together remaining soup, wine, and remaining shrimp. If desired, garnish with celery leaves.

6 servings

Tuna for Two, 42

Turbot Stuffed with Crab Meat

4 large turbot fillets (4 ounces each)
½ teaspoon salt
⅛ teaspoon pepper
1 package (6 ounces) frozen crab meat, thawed and flaked
1 can (10¾ ounces) condensed cream of mushroom soup
⅓ cup dry white wine
1 package (10 ounces) frozen mixed vegetables, cooked and drained

1. Sprinkle fillets with salt and pepper. Roll up, jelly-roll fashion. Place seam side down in a 1½-quart shallow casserole.
2. Combine soup, crab, wine, and vegetables. Spoon over fish.
3. Bake, covered, at 350°F 25 to 30 minutes, or until fish flakes when touched with a fork.

4 servings

Baked Flounder Superb

½ cup fine Melba toast crumbs
¼ cup butter or margarine, melted
⅔ cup minced green onion
2 tablespoons snipped parsley
½ teaspoon poultry seasoning
½ pound fresh or thawed frozen sea scallops, chopped
1 can (4 ounces) mushroom stems and pieces, drained
2 pounds fresh or frozen flounder fillets, cut in 12 pieces
2 tablespoons butter or margarine
2 tablespoons flour
¼ teaspoon salt
Few grains pepper
1 cup milk
Grated Parmesan cheese

1. Toss crumbs and melted butter together in a bowl. Add green onion, parsley, poultry seasoning, scallops, and mushrooms; mix well.
2. Place a piece of flounder in the bottom of each of 6 ramekins. Spoon stuffing mixture over flounder and top with remaining flounder pieces.
3. Melt remaining butter in a saucepan. Stir in flour, salt, and pepper. Gradually add milk, stirring until thickened and smooth.
4. Spoon sauce over flounder. Sprinkle with Parmesan cheese.
5. Bake, uncovered, at 350°F 20 to 25 minutes. If desired, set ramekins under broiler with tops about 3 inches from heat until lightly browned.

6 servings

BRUNCHES

Brunch is defined as a late breakfast, an early lunch, or a combination of the two. Recipes for omelets, soufflés, and other ways to prepare eggs with ease are found in this chapter. Also included are light meat dishes suitable for midday meals. Satisfying brunch casseroles let you start the new day right.

Baked Deviled Eggs

6 hard-cooked eggs
1¼ cups dairy sour cream
2 teaspoons prepared mustard
¼ teaspoon salt
½ cup chopped green pepper
¼ cup chopped onion
2 tablespoons butter or margarine
¼ cup chopped pimento
1 can (10¾ ounces) condensed cream
   of mushroom soup
½ cup (2 ounces) shredded Cheddar
   cheese
Paprika

1. Shell eggs and split in half lengthwise. Remove yolks; mash with fork. Combine with ¼ cup sour cream, mustard, and salt. Refill egg whites.
2. Sauté green pepper and onion in butter in a skillet. Stir in pimento, soup, and remaining 1 cup sour cream.
3. Pour into a 12x8-inch baking dish. Place deviled eggs on top, yolk side up. Sprinkle with cheese and paprika.
4. Bake, uncovered, at 325°F 25 minutes, or until heated through. Serve over **Holland rusks** with **hot cooked asparagus spears.**

6 servings

Brunch Egg Casserole

2 cups unflavored croutons
1 cup (4 ounces) shredded Cheddar
   cheese
4 eggs
2 cups milk
½ teaspoon salt
⅛ teaspoon onion powder
½ teaspoon prepared mustard
   Dash pepper
8 bacon slices, cooked, drained, and
   crumbled

1. Combine croutons and cheese. Place in bottom of a 10x6-inch baking dish.
2. Lightly beat together eggs, milk, salt, onion powder, mustard, and pepper. Pour over crouton-cheese mixture. Sprinkle bacon over top.
3. Bake, uncovered, at 325°F 55 to 60 minutes, or until set. Serve with **broiled tomato halves.**

6 servings

Brunch Cups

6 crepes (6 to 8 inches each)
½ cup chopped celery
2 tablespoons chopped green pepper
2 tablespoons chopped onion
3 tablespoons butter or margarine
2 cups chopped tomato
½ teaspoon salt
12 eggs
½ cup (2 ounces) shredded mozzarella
    cheese

1. Grease 6 individual 12-ounce (1½ cups) casseroles. Line each with a crepe.
2. Sauté celery, green pepper, and onion in butter in a skillet. Stir in tomato and salt. Cook over medium heat 5 minutes.
3. Divide tomato mixture evenly between the casseroles. Carefully break 2 eggs into each casserole over tomato mixture. Sprinkle each with cheese.
4. Bake, uncovered, at 325°F 25 to 30 minutes, or until eggs are done as desired. Serve with a sprinkling of **salt, pepper,** and **oregano.**

6 servings

Parmesan Baked Eggs

8 hard-cooked eggs
9 tablespoons butter or margarine
¼ cup flour
¼ teaspoon salt
¼ teaspoon white pepper
1½ cups milk
1 cup half-and-half
½ cup (2 ounces) shredded Swiss
    cheese
½ cup chopped fresh mushrooms
2 tablespoons chopped chives
2 tablespoons snipped parsley
2 tablespoons grated Parmesan cheese

1. Shell eggs and halve lengthwise. Remove yolks and mash with a fork. Set aside.
2. Melt 4 tablespoons of the butter in a saucepan. Stir in flour, salt, and pepper. Gradually add milk, stirring until thickened and smooth.
3. Add ¼ cup of this sauce to egg yolks. To remaining sauce, add half-and-half and Swiss cheese. Heat until cheese is melted and sauce is smooth.
4. Sauté mushrooms and chives in 4 tablespoons butter. Stir into egg-yolk mixture along with parsley. Fill egg whites with this mixture.
5. Spread one fourth of the sauce in a lightly greased 12x8-inch baking dish. Arrange eggs over sauce, yolk side up. Spoon on remaining sauce.
6. Sprinkle with Parmesan cheese. Dot with remaining 1 tablespoon butter.
7. Bake, uncovered, at 375°F 20 minutes, or until top is lightly browned.

8 servings

Sunnyside Eggs and Rice

½ cup chopped onion
½ cup chopped green pepper
1 tablespoon shortening*
4 cups cooked white rice
1 teaspoon Worcestershire sauce
¼ teaspoon pepper
1 tablespoon chopped pimento
1½ cups (6 ounces) shredded Cheddar
    cheese
6 eggs
6 slices bacon, cooked, drained, and
    crumbled

1. Sauté onion and green pepper in shortening in a skillet. Combine with rice, Worcestershire sauce, pepper, pimento, and 1 cup cheese.
2. Pack into a 10x6-inch baking dish. Make 6 indentations with back of spoon.
3. Break an egg into each indentation. Sprinkle with remaining ½ cup cheese and bacon.
4. Bake, covered, at 325°F 20 minutes, or until eggs are cooked to desired doneness. Serve with **broiled tomato halves.**

6 servings

* One tablespoon bacon drippings can be substituted for the shortening.

Company Ham-and-Egg Bake

12 hard-cooked eggs
3 cups chopped cooked ham
3 cups diced cooked potatoes
3 cans (10¾ ounces each) condensed ·
   cream of mushroom soup
½ cup milk
1 tablespoon Worcestershire sauce
1 tablespoon lemon juice
¼ cup snipped parsley

1. Shell eggs and halve lengthwise. Place eggs, yolk side up, in a 13x9-inch baking dish.
2. Spoon ham and potatoes over eggs.
3. Heat together soup, milk, Worcestershire sauce, and lemon juice. Pour over eggs. Sprinkle with parsley.
4. Bake, uncovered, at 350°F 30 minutes, or until heated through.

12 servings

Cheesy-Egg Bake

12 eggs, beaten
2 cans (17 ounces each) cream-style
   corn
4 cups (16 ounces) shredded Cheddar
   cheese
1 can (4 ounces) green chilies,
   drained and chopped
1 tablespoon Worcestershire sauce
1 tablespoon salt
½ teaspoon pepper

1. Combine all ingredients. Put into a 13x9-inch baking dish.
2. Bake, uncovered, at 325°F 1 hour and 15 minutes, or until set.

12 servings

Note: This casserole can be prepared and refrigerated overnight.

Baked Pineapple Toast

¼ cup butter or margarine, melted
½ cup firmly packed brown sugar
1 can (8 ounces) crushed pineapple,
   drained
6 white bread slices
2 eggs
1½ cups milk
½ teaspoon salt

1. Combine butter, brown sugar, and pineapple. Spread in bottom of a 13x9-inch baking dish. Top with bread.
2. Beat eggs, milk, and salt together. Pour over bread.
3. Bake, uncovered, at 325°F 25 minutes, or until golden brown. Cool slightly and invert on heated serving platter.

6 servings

Jalapeño Chili Pie

½ can (2 ounces) jalapeño chilies*
2 cups (8 ounces) shredded Cheddar
   cheese
4 eggs

1. Wash and remove membrane and seeds from chilies; chop. Sprinkle on bottom of a greased 10x6-inch baking dish. Top with cheese.
2. Lightly beat eggs. Pour over chili-cheese mixture.
3. Bake, uncovered, at 325°F 30 minutes, or until set. Cool about 15 minutes. Slice and serve with **stewed tomatoes** and **crisp bacon slices.**

4 servings

* For a spicier pie use the whole can of chilies.

Chicken and Ham Supreme

¼ **cup finely chopped onion**
1 **cup sliced fresh mushrooms**
2 **tablespoons butter or margarine**
1 **tablespoon flour**
½ **teaspoon paprika**
¼ **teaspoon salt**
¼ **teaspoon nutmeg**
1 **cup milk**
6 **slices cooked chicken**
½ **pound cubed cooked ham**
¼ **cup (1 ounce) grated Parmesan cheese**

1. Sauté onion and mushrooms in butter in a skillet. Stir in flour, paprika, salt, and nutmeg. Gradually add milk, stirring until thickened and smooth.
2. Arrange chicken and ham in a greased 1½-quart shallow baking dish. Top with sauce.
3. Bake, uncovered, at 350°F 15 minutes. Sprinkle with cheese and bake an additional 10 minutes, or until heated through.

6 servings

Puffy Cheese Casserole

½ **cup uncooked farina**
1 **teaspoon salt**
2½ **cups milk**
1 **cup (4 ounces) shredded American cheese**
1 **tablespoon butter or margarine**
3 **egg yolks, well beaten**
3 **egg whites, beaten stiff but not dry**

1. Combine farina, salt, and 1 cup milk.
2. Bring remaining 1½ cups milk to a boil. Slowly stir in farina mixture. Cook, stirring frequently, until thick (about 5 minutes).
3. Remove from heat. Add cheese and butter; stir until melted. Mix in egg yolks, then fold in egg whites. Put into a greased 1½-quart casserole.
4. Bake, uncovered, at 325°F 50 minutes, or until set.

6 servings

Roquefort Soufflé

2 **tablespoons butter or margarine**
3 **tablespoons flour**
¾ **cup milk**
1 **teaspoon snipped parsley**
½ **cup chopped onion**
½ **cup tomato juice**
6 **ounces Roquefort cheese**
½ **teaspoon salt**
¼ **teaspoon pepper**
½ **teaspoon dry mustard**
4 **eggs, separated**

1. Melt butter in a saucepan. Stir in flour. Gradually add milk, stirring until thickened and smooth.
2. Add parsley, onion, tomato juice, cheese, salt, pepper, and mustard. Stir until cheese is melted and sauce is smooth.
3. Remove from heat; beat in egg yolks.
4. Beat egg whites until stiff but not dry. Fold egg whites into sauce. Pour into a buttered and floured 1-quart soufflé dish.
5. Bake, uncovered, at 325°F 50 minutes, or until soufflé is lightly browned.

6 servings

Egg and Cheese Soufflé

6 white bread slices with crusts trimmed, lightly buttered and cubed
2 cups (8 ounces) shredded Cheddar cheese
1 cup sliced fresh mushrooms
4 eggs, well beaten
2 cups milk
½ teaspoon salt
  Dash pepper
½ teaspoon dry mustard

1. Layer half the bread cubes, half the cheese, and half the mushrooms in a buttered 1½-quart casserole; repeat layers.
2. Combine remaining ingredients. Pour into casserole. Cover and refrigerate 12 hours or overnight.
3. Remove from refrigerator 1 hour before baking.
4. Bake, uncovered, at 350°F 1 hour, or until puffed and brown.

6 servings*

* For 12 servings, double recipe and use a 3-quart casserole.

24-Hour Omelet

1 pound pork sausage meat
6 white bread slices, cubed
½ cup (2 ounces) shredded Cheddar cheese
1 package (3 ounces) cream cheese, cut in cubes
1 can (4 ounces) mushroom stems and pieces, drained
4 eggs
2 cups milk
1 teaspoon dry mustard
½ teaspoon salt
  Dash pepper

1. Brown sausage in a skillet; drain off excess fat.
2. Place bread cubes in a greased 2-quart shallow baking dish. Top with sausage, cheeses, and mushrooms.
3. Beat remaining ingredients together. Pour over mushrooms in casserole. Cover and refrigerate overnight.
4. Bake, covered, at 325°F 40 minutes. Uncover and continue baking 15 minutes, or until done.

6 to 8 servings

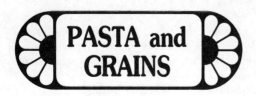

PASTA and GRAINS

By adding a few extra ingredients to noodles and rice, you'll find new enjoyment in these old favorites. Try these recipe ideas as a substitute where you would usually serve plain noodles, rice, or potatoes. Pasta and grain casseroles add a new dimension to meal planning because they can accompany any meat, poultry, or fish dish, and they taste extra good but don't require extra work in the kitchen.

Cheese Risotta

1 cup chopped onion
¼ cup butter or margarine
1 cup uncooked white rice
1 can (16 ounces) tomatoes
   (undrained)
1½ cups water
2 chicken bouillon cubes
1 can (3 ounces) mushroom slices,
   drained
   Dash pepper
   Few grains saffron (optional)
2 cups (8 ounces) shredded sharp
   Cheddar cheese

1. Sauté onion in butter in a skillet. Stir in rice; cook until lightly browned.
2. Add remaining ingredients, except cheese. Bring to a boil, stirring until bouillon cubes dissolve.
3. Place half the rice mixture in a 1½-quart casserole. Top with 1½ cups cheese. Evenly spoon remaining rice mixture over cheese.
4. Bake, covered, at 350°F 45 minutes, or until rice is tender. Remove cover; sprinkle with remaining ½ cup cheese. Bake an additional 5 minutes, or until cheese is melted.

6 servings

Baked Rice

1 cup uncooked white rice
1 can (5 ounces) water chestnuts,
   drained and sliced
2 cups boiling water
1 package (1⅜ ounces) dry onion
   soup mix
2 tablespoons chopped pimento

1. Place rice in bottom of a 1½-quart baking dish. Toast at 350°F 10 minutes, stirring occasionally until lightly browned.
2. Stir in remaining ingredients.
3. Bake, covered, at 350°F 45 minutes, or until rice is tender.

6 servings

Mushroom-Rice Casserole

1 cup uncooked white rice
½ cup slivered almonds
1 small onion, chopped
1 can (4 ounces) sliced mushrooms, drained*
¼ cup butter or margarine
2 cups water
2 chicken bouillon cubes
2 tablespoons lemon juice
1 teaspoon soy sauce
  Dash pepper
4 bacon slices, cooked and crumbled
2 tablespoons snipped parsley

1. Sauté rice, almonds, onion, and mushrooms in butter in a skillet. Stir in water, bouillon cubes, lemon juice, soy sauce, and pepper.
2. Heat to boiling. Cover and reduce heat to low. Cook until liquid is absorbed (about 20 minutes).
3. Stir in crumbled bacon and parsley. Put into a 1½-quart casserole.
4. Bake, covered, at 325°F 20 minutes, or until heated through.

6 servings

* The drained mushroom liquid can be used as part of the 2 cups water called for in the recipe.

Italian Rice Casserole

½ cup chopped onion
2 tablespoons oil
1 cup (4 ounces) shredded Cheddar cheese
1 cup sliced fresh mushrooms
¾ cup sliced pitted ripe olives
1 can (16 ounces) stewed tomatoes
1½ cups boiling water
1 package (6 ounces) long-grain and wild rice mix

1. Sauté onion in oil in a skillet. Combine with remaining ingredients. Put into a 2-quart baking dish.
2. Bake, covered, at 350°F 1 hour, or until rice is tender.

6 servings

Rice Loaf

2 cups cooked brown rice
½ cup finely chopped onion
½ cup finely chopped pecans
2 tablespoons snipped parsley
½ teaspoon salt
¼ teaspoon thyme
½ cup milk
1 egg, well beaten

1. Combine all ingredients. Put into a 1-quart casserole.
2. Bake, uncovered, at 350°F 35 to 40 minutes, or until set.

6 servings

Brunch Pilaf

1 package (6 ounces) long-grain and
    wild rice mix
½ pound pork sausage links, cut in
    1-inch pieces
½ pound fresh mushrooms, sliced
3 tablespoons butter or margarine
½ teaspoon salt
¼ teaspoon pepper
2 teaspoons instant minced onion
½ pound chicken livers, cut up

1. Prepare rice according to package directions.
2. Brown sausage in a skillet about 15 minutes. Drain and set aside.
3. Sauté mushrooms in 2 tablespoons butter. Toss with ¼ teaspoon salt, pepper, and minced onion; set aside.
4. Sauté chicken livers in remaining 1 tablespoon butter until lightly browned. Sprinkle with remaining ¼ teaspoon salt.
5. Combine all ingredients and put into a 1½-quart casserole.
6. Bake, covered, at 325°F 30 minutes, or until heated through.

6 to 8 servings

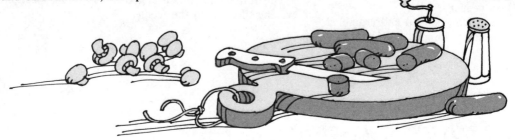

Mushroom Wild Rice

1 package (4 ounces) wild rice
1 medium green pepper, chopped
1 large onion, chopped
½ cup chopped celery
¼ cup butter or margarine
1 egg, beaten
1 can (10¾ ounces) condensed cream
    of mushroom soup
¼ cup sliced almonds
2 tablespoons snipped parsley

1. Prepare rice according to package directions.
2. Sauté green pepper, onion, and celery in butter in a skillet. Add to rice along with beaten egg. Put into a greased 1½-quart casserole.
3. Top with mushroom soup; mix slightly. Sprinkle with almonds.
4. Bake, covered, at 350°F 30 minutes, or until heated through. Sprinkle with parsley.

6 servings

Wild Rice Casserole

1 cup wild rice
2 tablespoons chopped onion
½ pound fresh mushrooms, sliced
½ cup butter or margarine
3 cups broth*
1 teaspoon salt
½ cup toasted slivered almonds

1. Sauté rice, onion, and mushrooms in butter in a skillet. Add broth and salt. Pour into a 1½-quart casserole.
2. Bake, covered, at 325°F 1 hour. Remove cover; top with almonds. Bake an additional 15 minutes, or until rice is tender. If desired, top with fresh tomato wedges.

6 servings

* Use beef broth when serving with meat and chicken broth when serving with poultry.

Egg Noodle Supreme

2 cups cooked noodles
¼ cup finely chopped green onion
1 garlic clove, minced
½ teaspoon tarragon
½ cup (2 ounces) shredded Colby
    cheese
½ cup milk
1 tablespoon butter or margarine,
    melted
½ cup dairy sour cream

1. Combine all ingredients, except sour cream. Put into a 1-quart casserole.
2. Bake, covered, at 350°F 25 minutes. Remove cover; stir in sour cream. Bake an additional 5 minutes, or until heated through.

4 servings

Noodles au Gratin

1 small onion, chopped
¼ cup butter or margarine
4 cups noodles, cooked and drained
½ cup dairy sour cream
6 slices (1 ounce each) American
    cheese, cut in pieces
½ teaspoon salt
½ cup milk
    Paprika

1. Sauté onion in butter in a skillet. Combine with noodles, sour cream, cheese, and salt. Put into a 1½-quart casserole.
2. Pour milk over all. Sprinkle with paprika.
3. Bake, covered, at 350°F 40 minutes, or until golden brown.

6 to 8 servings

Noodles Romanoff

4 cups noodles, cooked and drained
1½ cups (12 ounces) cream-style
    cottage cheese
1 cup dairy sour cream
¼ cup finely chopped onion
1 teaspoon Worcestershire sauce
½ teaspoon salt
¼ teaspoon white pepper
½ cup (2 ounces) shredded Cheddar
    cheese
2 tablespoons snipped parsley

1. Combine all ingredients, except Cheddar cheese and parsley. Put into a 2-quart casserole. Sprinkle with cheese.
2. Bake, covered, at 325°F 40 minutes, or until heated through. Sprinkle with parsley.

6 servings

Spaghetti Fromaggi

¼ cup chopped onion
¼ cup chopped green pepper
¼ cup butter or margarine
¼ cup flour
1 teaspoon salt
¼ teaspoon pepper
3½ cups milk
1 cup (4 ounces) shredded Swiss
   cheese
1 cup (4 ounces) shredded Cheddar
   cheese
1 tablespoon Worcestershire sauce
1 tablespoon chopped pimento
1 package (16 ounces) spaghetti,
   cooked and drained
1 tablespoon snipped parsley

1. Sauté onion and green pepper in butter in a skillet. Stir in flour, salt, and pepper. Gradually add milk, stirring until thickened and smooth.
2. Stir in cheeses, Worcestershire sauce, pimento, and spaghetti. Put into a 3-quart casserole.
3. Bake, covered, at 350°F 45 minutes, or until heated through. Sprinkle with parsley.

8 servings

Barley Italienne

6 bacon slices, cut in 1-inch pieces
1½ cups quick-cooking barley
2¼ cups water
1 can (16 ounces) tomatoes
   (undrained)
1 can (8 ounces) tomato sauce
1 medium onion, sliced
1 garlic clove, minced
2 teaspoons salt
½ teaspoon oregano
¼ teaspoon pepper
8 ounces American cheese, sliced

1. Fry bacon in a skillet; drain off excess fat, reserving 2 tablespoons drippings.
2. Brown barley in bacon drippings in skillet. Add water and tomatoes. Bring to a boil; reduce heat. Cover and simmer 10 to 12 minutes, stirring occasionally.
3. Add bacon and remaining ingredients, except cheese. Cover and cook an additional 5 minutes.
4. Layer barley mixture and cheese alternately in a greased 2-quart casserole, ending with cheese on top.
5. Bake, covered, at 350°F 10 to 12 minutes, or until cheese is melted and mixture is heated through.

6 servings

Barley-Mushroom Casserole

½ cup finely chopped onion
½ pound fresh mushrooms, sliced
¼ cup butter or margarine
2 beef bouillon cubes
1 quart boiling water
1 teaspoon salt
1 cup barley

1. Sauté onion and mushrooms in butter in a skillet.
2. Dissolve bouillon cubes in boiling water. Mix with salt, barley, onion, and mushrooms. Pour into a 2-quart casserole.
3. Bake, uncovered, at 350°F 1 hour, stirring occasionally. Cover and bake an additional 30 minutes, or until barley is tender.

6 servings

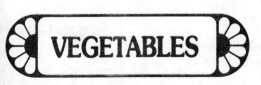

VEGETABLES

Artichokes, broccoli, carrots, potatoes, zucchini. Practically any vegetable can be prepared casserole style. By adding special seasonings or by combining different vegetables, you can create side dishes that will tempt even those people who usually refuse vegetables. Vegetable casseroles take only minutes to prepare and cook, and will complement any meal from hamburgers to roast turkey.

Layered Casserole

1 can (14½ ounces) asparagus spears, drained
1 can (17 ounces) green peas
1 can (8½ ounces) water chestnuts, drained and sliced
2 tablespoons chopped pimento
½ cup fine dry bread crumbs
1 can (10¾ ounces) condensed cream of mushroom soup
½ cup (2 ounces) shredded American cheese

1. Arrange asparagus spears in bottom of a 1½-quart shallow baking dish.
2. Drain peas, reserving ¼ cup liquid. Top asparagus spears with peas, water chestnuts, and pimento. Sprinkle with ¼ cup bread crumbs.
3. Combine soup with reserved ¼ cup pea liquid. Evenly spread over bread crumbs. Sprinkle with remaining ¼ cup bread crumbs and cheese.
4. Bake, uncovered, at 350°F 20 minutes, or until heated through.

6 servings

Marinated Artichoke Hearts Supreme

2 jars (6 ounces each) marinated artichoke hearts
1 garlic clove, minced
½ cup chopped onion
4 eggs, beaten
¼ cup fine dry bread crumbs
2 tablespoons snipped parsley
½ teaspoon salt
½ teaspoon oregano
¼ teaspoon pepper
¼ teaspoon Tabasco
2 cups (8 ounces) shredded Cheddar cheese

1. Cut up artichoke hearts, reserving liquid from 1 jar.
2. Pour liquid into a skillet and sauté garlic and onion.
3. Combine with eggs, bread crumbs, parsley, salt, oregano, pepper, and Tabasco. Stir in cheese and artichoke hearts. Pour into a greased 1½-quart shallow baking dish.
4. Bake, uncovered, at 325°F 30 minutes, or until set.

6 servings

Sweet-and-Sour Green Beans

8 bacon slices, cut in 1-inch pieces
½ cup sugar
1 tablespoon cornstarch
1 cup vinegar
1 large onion, thinly sliced
2 cans (16 ounces each) cut green
  beans, drained

1. Fry bacon in a skillet.
2. Combine sugar and cornstarch. Blend in vinegar. Add to bacon and drippings in a skillet, stirring until thickened.
3. Put onion and beans into a 1½-quart casserole. Stir in vinegar mixture.
4. Bake, covered, at 300°F 1 hour, stirring once.

6 servings

Spicy Lima Beans

6 bacon slices, cut up
½ cup chopped onion
2 tablespoons flour
¼ teaspoon salt
  Dash pepper
1 bay leaf
1 can (16 ounces) tomatoes
  (undrained)
2 packages (10 ounces each) frozen
  lima beans, cooked and drained
½ cup fine dry bread crumbs
2 tablespoons butter or margarine,
  melted

1. Fry bacon and onion in a skillet. Stir in flour, salt, pepper, and bay leaf. Gradually add tomatoes and juice, stirring until thickened.
2. Add lima beans. Put into a 1½-quart casserole.
3. Combine bread crumbs and butter. Sprinkle over beans.
4. Bake, covered, at 350°F 20 minutes. Remove cover and bay leaf. Bake an additional 10 minutes, or until heated through.

6 servings

Broccoli Casserole

¼ cup chopped onion
¼ cup butter or margarine
2 teaspoons flour
½ cup water
1 jar (8 ounces) pasteurized process
  cheese spread
2 packages (10 ounces each) frozen
  chopped broccoli, thawed and
  squeezed
3 eggs, well beaten
½ cup buttered bread crumbs

1. Sauté onion in butter in a skillet. Stir in flour. Gradually add water, stirring until thickened and smooth.
2. Blend in cheese until melted. Combine with broccoli and eggs. Pour into a greased 1½-quart casserole. Sprinkle with bread crumbs.
3. Bake, uncovered, at 350°F 45 minutes, or until set.

6 servings

Broccoli Bake

2 packages (10 ounces each) frozen
    chopped broccoli, cooked and
    drained
1 can (10¾ ounces) condensed cream
    of mushroom soup
½ cup mayonnaise
1 cup (4 ounces) shredded Cheddar
    cheese
1 tablespoon lemon juice
½ cup crumbled cheese crackers

1. Spread broccoli in bottom of 10x6-inch baking dish.
2. Combine soup, mayonnaise, cheese, and lemon juice. Spread over broccoli. Sprinkle with cracker crumbs.
3. Bake, uncovered, at 350°F 30 minutes, or until heated through.

6 servings

Broccoli-Mushroom Casserole

1 package (10 ounces) frozen chopped
    broccoli, cooked and drained
1 can (4 ounces) mushroom slices,
    drained
2 tablespoons chopped pimento
⅓ cup dairy sour cream
½ cup chopped celery
½ teaspoon salt
    Dash pepper

1. Combine all ingredients. Put into a 1-quart casserole.
2. Bake, covered, at 350°F 25 minutes, or until heated through.

3 servings

Brussels Sprouts in Broth

2 packages (10 ounces each) frozen
    Brussels sprouts, cooked and
    drained
1 cup water
1 beef bouillon cube
2 tablespoons butter or margarine
½ cup (2 ounces) freshly grated
    Parmesan cheese

1. Put Brussels sprouts into a 1-quart casserole.
2. Heat together water, bouillon cube, and butter. Pour over Brussels sprouts. Sprinkle with cheese.
3. Bake, covered, at 325°F 20 minutes, or until heated through.

6 servings

Note: To improve flavor, cover and refrigerate Brussels sprouts, broth, and butter overnight. Add cheese before baking.

Carrot-Apricot Casserole

1 package (11 ounces) dried apricots
1 can (12 ounces) apricot nectar
2 jars (16 ounces each) tiny whole Belgian carrots, drained
½ cup firmly packed brown sugar
4 tablespoons butter or margarine
¼ cup slivered almonds

1. Soak apricots in nectar overnight.
2. Put 1 jar carrots into a 2-quart casserole. Top with half the apricots, half the apricot nectar, and ¼ cup brown sugar.
3. Dot with 2 tablespoons butter; repeat layers. Sprinkle with almonds.
4. Bake, covered, at 350°F 30 minutes, or until bubbly.

8 servings

Marmalade Carrots

4 cups thinly sliced carrots
⅓ cup orange juice
½ teaspoon salt
¼ teaspoon ginger
⅓ cup orange marmalade
1 tablespoon butter or margarine

1. Combine carrots, orange juice, salt, ginger, and marmalade.
2. Put into a 1½-quart casserole. Dot with butter.
3. Bake, covered, at 350°F 30 minutes, or until carrots are tender. If desired, sprinkle with snipped parsley.

8 servings

Brandied Carrots

4 cups thinly sliced carrots
¼ cup butter or margarine
¼ cup water
1 teaspoon lemon juice
½ teaspoon salt
¼ teaspoon pepper
¼ cup brandy
2 tablespoons snipped parsley

1. Put carrots into a large saucepan. Add butter and water. Cover and cook over moderate heat, stirring occasionally, until carrots are just crisp-tender (about 15 minutes).
2. Add lemon juice, salt, pepper, and brandy.
3. Put into a 1½-quart casserole. Cover and refrigerate overnight.
4. Bake, covered, at 350°F 30 minutes, or until heated through. Sprinkle with parsley.

8 servings

Baked Deviled Eggs, 51

Cabbage Casserole

1 head cabbage, cut in 6 wedges
1½ cups (6 ounces) shredded Cheddar
    cheese
¼ cup butter or margarine
¼ cup flour
½ teaspoon seasoned salt
½ teaspoon sugar
⅛ teaspoon garlic powder
1¾ cups milk

1. Cook cabbage in **boiling salted water** about 10 minutes, or until tender.
2. Layer cabbage and 1 cup cheese in a 2-quart casserole.
3. Melt butter in a saucepan. Stir in flour, seasoned salt, sugar, and garlic powder. Gradually add milk, stirring until thickened and smooth.
4. Pour over cabbage. Sprinkle with remaining ½ cup cheese.
5. Bake, covered, at 350°F 20 minutes, or until heated through. If desired, sprinkle with paprika.

6 servings

Sour Red Cabbage

1 head red cabbage, shredded
1 onion, finely chopped
2 cooking apples, cored and cut up
¼ cup red wine vinegar
¼ cup water
1 tablespoon firmly packed brown
    sugar
1 teaspoon salt
¼ teaspoon pepper
1 tablespoon butter

1. Combine all ingredients, except butter.
2. Put into a 2-quart casserole. Dot with butter.
3. Bake, covered, at 350°F 1 hour, or until cabbage is tender.

6 servings

Scalloped Corn and Broccoli

¼ cup chopped onion
2 tablespoons butter or margarine
1 tablespoon flour
1¼ cups milk*
1 cup (4 ounces) shredded Cheddar
    cheese
1 can (12 ounces) whole kernel corn,
    drained
2 packages (10 ounces each) frozen
    broccoli spears, cooked and
    drained

1. Sauté onion in butter in a skillet. Stir in flour. Gradually add milk, stirring until thickened and smooth.
2. Add cheese, stirring until melted. Stir in corn.
3. Arrange broccoli in a 2-quart shallow baking dish.
4. Pour corn sauce over broccoli.
5. Bake, uncovered, at 350°F 30 minutes, or until heated through.

8 servings

* One-fourth cup of the drained corn liquid can be substituted for ¼ cup of the milk.

Lemon Crunch Dessert, 74

Creole Eggplant

1 eggplant
1¼ teaspoons salt
2 tablespoons butter or margarine
2 tablespoons flour
1 can (28 ounces) tomatoes
    (undrained)
½ cup chopped onion
½ cup chopped green pepper
2 tablespoons firmly packed brown
    sugar
¼ teaspoon pepper
¼ cup buttered bread crumbs

1. Pare and cut eggplant into cubes. Sprinkle with 1 teaspoon salt. Let stand 15 minutes.
2. Rinse and drain eggplant. Cook in **boiling water** 10 minutes; drain. Put into a 1½-quart casserole.
3. Melt butter in a saucepan. Stir in flour. Gradually add tomatoes and liquid, stirring until thickened.
4. Add onion, green pepper, brown sugar, pepper, and the remaining ¼ teaspoon salt. Pour over eggplant.
5. Bake, covered, at 350°F 15 minutes. Remove cover; sprinkle with bread crumbs. Bake an additional 5 minutes, or until heated through.

4 to 6 servings

Italian Eggplant Casserole

1 large eggplant
¼ cup milk
1 egg, beaten
½ cup fine dry bread crumbs
1 teaspoon salt
¼ cup shortening
1 can (8 ounces) tomato paste
1 can (8 ounces) spaghetti sauce
8 ounces mozzarella cheese, thinly
    sliced
½ cup (2 ounces) grated Parmesan
    cheese

1. Pare eggplant and cut into ¼-inch slices.
2. Combine milk and egg. Also combine bread crumbs and salt.
3. Dip eggplant into milk mixture, then bread crumbs. Fry eggplant in shortening in a skillet. Drain on absorbent paper.
4. Combine tomato paste and spaghetti sauce.
5. Alternate layers of half the eggplant, half the sauce, and half the mozzarella cheese in a 2-quart casserole. Repeat layers. Sprinkle with Parmesan cheese.
6. Bake, covered, at 350°F 30 minutes, or until heated through.

8 servings

Carrot Soufflé

3 tablespoons butter or margarine
3 tablespoons flour
1 cup milk
1 teaspoon sugar
½ teaspoon salt
¼ teaspoon pepper
2 cups mashed cooked carrots (about 1 pound fresh)
3 eggs, separated

1. Melt butter in a saucepan. Stir in flour. Gradually add milk, stirring until thickened and smooth.
2. Blend in sugar, salt, pepper, and mashed carrots. Beat in egg yolks.
3. Beat egg whites until stiff but not dry. Fold in carrot mixture. Divide in 2 buttered 1½-quart casseroles.
4. Bake, uncovered, in hot water bath at 325°F 50 minutes, or until set.

8 servings

Vegetable Spoon Bread

1 cup cornmeal
1½ teaspoons salt
1 cup cold milk
1½ cups milk, scalded
1 tablespoon butter or margarine
1 can (16 ounces) mixed vegetables, drained
5 bacon slices, cooked and crumbled
4 egg yolks
4 egg whites, beaten stiff but not dry

1. Combine cornmeal, salt, and cold milk. Add to scalded milk. Cook until thickened (about 5 minutes), stirring constantly.
2. Remove from heat; add butter, vegetables, and bacon.
3. Beat egg yolks until thick and lemon colored. Stir a small amount of cornmeal mixture into egg yolks; add egg mixture to cornmeal, stirring constantly. Fold in beaten egg white.
4. Pour into a greased 2-quart casserole or soufflé dish.
5. Bake, uncovered, at 350°F 50 to 60 minutes, or until set. Serve immediately.

6 servings

Mushroom Business

1 pound fresh mushrooms, thickly
   sliced
¼ cup butter or margarine
7 slices white bread, buttered
½ cup chopped onion
½ cup chopped celery
½ cup chopped green pepper
½ cup mayonnaise
¾ teaspoon salt
¼ teaspoon pepper
2 eggs, slightly beaten
1½ cups milk
1 can (10¾ ounces) condensed cream
   of mushroom soup
1 tablespoon grated Parmesan cheese

1. Sauté mushrooms in butter in a skillet; set aside.
2. Cut 3 slices bread into 1-inch cubes. Put into a 2½-quart casserole.
3. Combine mushrooms, onion, celery, green pepper, mayonnaise, salt, and pepper. Spoon on top of bread cubes.
4. Cut 3 slices bread into 1-inch cubes and put onto mushroom mixture.
5. Combine eggs and milk. Pour over mushroom mixture. Cover and refrigerate at least 1 hour.
6. Remove from refrigerator; uncover and spoon soup overall.
7. Cut remaining slice bread into 1-inch cubes; arrange over soup. Sprinkle with Parmesan cheese.
8. Bake, uncovered, at 300°F 60 to 70 minutes, or until mixture is set.

8 servings

Broccoli-Stuffed Onions

3 medium sweet Spanish onions
2 tablespoons butter or margarine
2 tablespoons flour
¼ teaspoon salt
1 cup milk
1 package (3 ounces) cream cheese,
   cut in cubes
1 package (10 ounces) frozen chopped
   broccoli, cooked and drained
½ cup (2 ounces) grated Parmesan
   cheese
1 teaspoon lemon juice

1. Peel and halve onions. Cook in **boiling salted water** 10 minutes; drain. Remove centers, leaving a ½-inch edge. Chop center portion to equal ½ cup.*
2. Melt butter in a saucepan. Stir in flour and salt. Gradually add milk, stirring until thickened and smooth. Add cream cheese, stirring until smooth.
3. Stir in broccoli, Parmesan cheese, lemon juice, and chopped onion. Spoon into onion halves. Place in a 2-quart shallow baking dish.
4. Bake, uncovered, at 375°F 20 minutes, or until heated through.

6 servings

* Use remaining onion in other casserole mixtures.

Barbecue Potatoes

8 potatoes
3 tablespoons flour
2¼ cups water
¾ cup barbecue sauce
1 tablespoon vinegar
2 teaspoons salt
2 small onions, thinly sliced
   Paprika
1 tablespoon snipped parsley

1. Pare and thinly slice potatoes. Sprinkle with flour.
2. Combine water, barbecue sauce, vinegar, and salt in a large saucepan. Stir in potato and onion. Simmer 5 minutes, stirring frequently.
3. Pour into a 3-quart casserole.
4. Bake, covered, at 350°F 1 hour, or until potatoes are tender. Sprinkle with paprika and parsley.

8 servings

Mashed Potato Casserole

2 pounds potatoes
⅓ to ½ cup milk
¼ cup butter or margarine
¼ cup chopped green pepper
1 package (3 ounces) cream cheese,
    cut in cubes
½ cup dairy sour cream
1 teaspoon salt
1 teaspoon onion salt
    Dash pepper

1. Cook potatoes in **boiling water;** drain. Mash with milk and butter.
2. Beat in remaining ingredients. Put into a 1½-quart casserole.
3. Bake, covered, at 350°F 40 minutes, or until heated through. Garnish with **parsley** and **paprika.**

6 servings

Potato-Mushroom Casserole

3 cups sliced potatoes (about 4
    medium)
1 cup sliced fresh mushrooms
1 onion, thinly sliced
3 beef bouillon cubes
1½ cups boiling water
¼ teaspoon salt
¼ teaspoon thyme
    Dash pepper

1. Put potatoes, mushrooms, and onion into a 1½-quart casserole.
2. Dissolve bouillon cubes in boiling water. Add salt, thyme, and pepper. Pour over vegetables.
3. Bake, covered, at 350°F 30 minutes. Remove cover and bake an additional 15 minutes, or until vegetables are tender.

6 servings

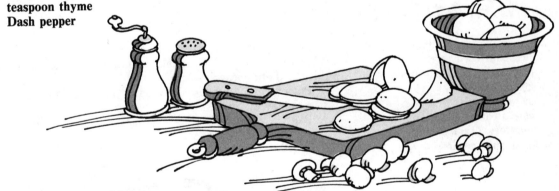

Potato Stuffing

2 cups chopped pared potatoes
¼ cup butter or margarine
1 medium apple, chopped
¾ cup chopped onion
1 garlic clove, minced
2 tablespoons snipped parsley
1 cup unflavored croutons
1½ teaspoons salt
1 egg, beaten
½ cup milk

1. Sauté potatoes in butter in a skillet 10 minutes, or until lightly browned.
2. Add remaining ingredients. Put into a 1½-quart casserole.
3. Bake, covered, at 325°F 30 minutes, or until heated through.

6 servings

Deluxe Scalloped Potatoes

1 package (5.5 ounces) scalloped
    potatoes
2 tablespoons butter or margarine
2½ cups boiling water
⅔ cup milk
⅓ cup crumbled blue cheese

1. Empty potato slices into a 1½-quart casserole. Sprinkle with sauce mix.
2. Stir in butter, water, milk, and blue cheese.
3. Bake, uncovered, at 400°F 30 to 35 minutes, or until potatoes are tender. Let stand a few minutes before serving.

4 servings

Apple-Honey Sweet Potatoes

4 sweet potatoes
4 cooking apples
½ cup honey
¼ teaspoon nutmeg

1. Bake sweet potatoes at 350°F 45 minutes, or until tender.
2. Core apples and cut into thin slices. (To avoid darkening, brush with lemon juice.)
3. Peel baked potatoes and cut into ½-inch-thick slices.
4. Alternate layers of potatoes and apples in a greased 2½-quart casserole. Drizzle with honey and sprinkle with nutmeg.
5. Bake, covered, at 350°F 20 minutes, or until heated through.

6 servings

Pecan Sweet Potatoes

¼ cup butter or margarine
2 tablespoons cornstarch
¾ cup firmly packed brown sugar
½ teaspoon salt
2 cups orange juice
2 cans (23 ounces each) sweet
    potatoes, drained
¼ cup chopped pecans

1. Melt butter in a saucepan. Blend cornstarch, brown sugar, and salt; mix with butter. Gradually add orange juice, stirring until thickened and clear.
2. Put sweet potatoes into a 1½-quart casserole. Pour sauce over sweet potatoes. Sprinkle with pecans.
3. Bake, covered, at 350°F 45 minutes, or until heated through.

8 servings

Spinach Bake

- 2 packages (10 ounces each) frozen chopped spinach, thawed and drained
- 2 cups milk
- 6 eggs
- ½ teaspoon salt
- 1 tablespoon instant minced onion
- ¾ cup (3 ounces) shredded Swiss cheese

1. Blend spinach, milk, eggs, and salt in a blender.
2. Pour into an 8-inch square baking dish. Sprinkle with onion and cheese.
3. Bake, uncovered, at 325°F 45 minutes, or until set. Let stand a few minutes. Cut into squares to serve.

6 servings

Spinach-Artichoke Casserole

- 1 jar (6 ounces) marinated artichoke hearts, drained
- 2 packages (10 ounces each) frozen chopped spinach, cooked and squeezed
- 1 package (8 ounces) cream cheese, softened
- 2 tablespoons butter or margarine, softened
- ¼ cup milk
- ½ teaspoon freshly ground pepper
- ¼ cup (1 ounce) grated Parmesan cheese

1. Put artichoke hearts into a 1½-quart casserole.
2. Spread spinach over artichoke hearts.
3. Beat together cream cheese and butter. Gradually add milk, beating until smooth. Spread over spinach.
4. Sprinkle pepper and Parmesan cheese over top.
5. Bake, covered, at 350°F 30 minutes. Remove cover. Garnish with **pimento strips** and **hard-cooked egg slices**. Bake an additional 10 minutes, or until heated through.

6 servings

Spinach and Rice

- 1 package (10 ounces) frozen chopped spinach, cooked and drained
- 1 can (10¾ ounces) condensed cream of mushroom soup
- 1½ cups boiling water
- 1⅓ cups packaged precooked rice
- ⅛ teaspoon garlic powder
- 1 teaspoon lemon juice
- 2 hard-cooked eggs, sliced
- ¾ cup (3 ounces) shredded Cheddar cheese
- 1 can (3 ounces) French-fried onions

1. Combine spinach, soup, boiling water, rice, garlic powder, and lemon juice. Put into a 1½-quart shallow baking dish.
2. Bake, covered, at 400°F 25 minutes, or until rice is tender. Remove cover and stir. Arrange eggs over top. Sprinkle with cheese. Place onions around edge. Bake an additional 5 minutes, or until cheese is melted.

4 servings

Spinach Pudding

¼ **cup chopped onion**
¼ **cup chopped green pepper**
2 **tablespoons butter or margarine**
1 **tablespoon flour**
1 **teaspoon salt**
1 **cup milk**
2 **packages (10 ounces each) frozen chopped spinach, cooked and drained**
2 **eggs, well beaten**

1. Sauté onion and green pepper in butter in a skillet. Stir in flour and salt. Gradually add milk, stirring until thickened and smooth. Remove from heat.
2. Stir in spinach and eggs. Pour into a greased 1-quart casserole. Set casserole in pan of hot water 1 inch deep.
3. Bake, uncovered, at 350°F 30 minutes, or until set. If desired, garnish with pimento strips.

6 servings

Layered Tomato Casserole

1 **cup sliced celery**
4 **tablespoons butter or margarine**
¾ **teaspoon basil**
½ **teaspoon salt**
¼ **teaspoon pepper**
3 **tomatoes, sliced**
1 **large onion, sliced**
1 **garlic clove, minced**
⅓ **cup fine dry bread crumbs**

1. Put celery into a 1½-quart casserole.
2. Dot with 1 tablespoon butter. Sprinkle with a little basil, a little salt, and a dash of pepper. Repeat with a layer of tomatoes and a layer of onion.
3. Sauté garlic in remaining 1 tablespoon butter. Stir in bread crumbs. Sprinkle over onion.
4. Bake, covered, at 350°F 30 minutes, or until vegetables are tender.

6 servings

Baked Tomato Pudding

1 **can (20 ounces) tomatoes (undrained)**
⅔ **cup firmly packed brown sugar**
1 **teaspoon salt**
½ **cup water**
4 **slices white bread, cut in ½-inch cubes (about 3 cups)**
½ **cup butter or margarine, melted**

1. Force tomatoes through a sieve into a saucepan; add brown sugar, salt, and water. Bring to a boil; boil 5 minutes.
2. Put bread crumbs into a 1½-quart casserole. Pour melted butter over bread cubes. Add tomato mixture and stir.
3. Bake, uncovered, at 350°F 45 minutes.

6 servings

Honey-Glazed Turnips

6 white turnips
1 cup chicken broth
3 tablespoons honey
¼ teaspoon salt
¼ teaspoon white pepper
  Paprika

1. Pare and slice turnips.
2. Bring broth to a boil in a large saucepan. Add turnips; boil, covered, 5 minutes. Remove cover and continue cooking over low heat until most of liquid has evaporated.
3. Add honey, salt, and pepper. Put into a 1½-quart casserole. Cover and refrigerate overnight.
4. Bake, covered, at 350°F 30 minutes, or until heated through. If desired, sprinkle with snipped parsley.

6 servings

Sue's Best Zucchini

4 small zucchini, thinly sliced
¾ cup shredded carrot
½ cup chopped onion
6 tablespoons butter or margarine, melted
2½ cups herb stuffing cubes
1 can (10¾ ounces) condensed cream of mushroom soup
½ cup dairy sour cream

1. Combine all ingredients. Put into a 1½-quart casserole.
2. Bake, covered, at 350°F 30 to 40 minutes, or until zucchini is tender, stirring once.

6 servings

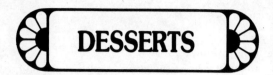

DESSERTS

Dessert casseroles are a perfect end to your meals. While the main course is being enjoyed, the dessert is ready to be served. Easy and delicious from warm puddings to cooled custards. Shouldn't all desserts be like that?

Lemon Crunch Dessert

Lemon mixture:
- ¾ cup sugar
- 2 tablespoons flour
- ⅛ teaspoon salt
- 1 cup water
- 2 eggs, well beaten
- 1 teaspoon grated lemon peel
- ⅓ cup lemon juice

Crunch mixture:
- ½ cup butter or margarine
- 1 cup firmly packed brown sugar
- 1 cup all-purpose flour
- ½ teaspoon salt
- 1 cup whole wheat flakes, crushed
- ½ cup finely chopped walnuts
- ½ cup shredded coconut

1. For lemon mixture, mix sugar, flour, and salt in a heavy saucepan. Gradually add water, stirring until smooth. Bring mixture to boiling and cook 2 minutes.
2. Stir about 3 tablespoons of the hot mixture vigorously into beaten eggs. Immediately blend into mixture in saucepan. Cook and stir about 3 minutes.
3. Remove from heat and stir in lemon peel and lemon juice. Set aside to cool.
4. For crunch mixture, beat butter until softened; add brown sugar gradually, beating until fluffy. Add flour and salt; mix well. Add wheat flakes, walnuts, and coconut; mix thoroughly.
5. Line bottom of an 8-inch square baking dish with one third of the crunch mixture. Cover with the lemon mixture, spreading to form an even layer. Top with remaining crunch mixture.
6. Bake, uncovered, at 350°F 40 minutes, or until lightly browned. Serve warm or cold.

8 servings

Hot Spicy Fruit Pot

- 1 can (16 ounces) pear halves
- 1 can (16 ounces) peach halves
- 1 can (16 ounces) purple plums, halved and pitted
- 1 cup firmly packed brown sugar
- 1 cinnamon stick
- ¼ teaspoon nutmeg
- ¼ teaspoon allspice
- ⅛ teaspoon ginger
- ¼ cup lemon juice
- 2 teaspoons grated orange peel
- 2 tablespoons butter or margarine

1. Drain fruits, reserving 1 cup liquid. Put fruit into a buttered 2-quart casserole.
2. Combine reserved liquid with remaining ingredients, except butter. Pour over fruit. Dot with butter.
3. Bake, covered, at 350°F 30 minutes, or until bubbly. Serve hot or cold. If desired, spoon over ice cream or cake.

8 servings

Buttery Baked Apples

8 medium baking apples, cored
1 cup sugar
6 tablespoons butter or margarine
1 tablespoon cornstarch
1 tablespoon cold water
½ teaspoon vanilla extract
½ cup milk

1. Put apples into a 1½-quart baking dish. Sprinkle with sugar. Dot with butter.
2. Bake, uncovered, at 450°F 20 minutes, or until fork-tender, basting occasionally.
3. Remove baking dish from oven and apples from baking dish.
4. Combine cornstarch, water, and vanilla extract; add to milk. Stir into liquid in baking dish. Return apples to baking dish.
5. Bake an additional 8 to 10 minutes, or until sauce is thickened. To serve, spoon sauce over each apple.

8 servings

Cherry-Pineapple Cobbler

1 can (21 ounces) cherry pie filling
1 can (13¼ ounces) pineapple tidbits, drained
¼ teaspoon allspice
3 tablespoons honey
1 egg, slightly beaten
½ cup dairy sour cream
1½ cups unflavored croutons

1. Combine cherry pie filling, pineapple tidbits, allspice, and 1 tablespoon honey. Put into a 1½-quart baking dish.
2. Blend egg, sour cream, and remaining 2 tablespoons honey. Stir in croutons. Spoon over cherry-pineapple mixture.
3. Bake, uncovered, at 375°F 30 minutes, or until heated through. If desired, top with ice cream.

8 servings

Indian Pudding

3 cups milk
½ cup cornmeal
1 tablespoon butter or margarine
½ cup light molasses
½ teaspoon salt
½ teaspoon ginger
1 cup cold milk

1. Scald 2½ cups milk in top of double boiler over boiling water.
2. Combine cornmeal and the remaining ½ cup milk. Add to scalded milk, stirring constantly. Cook about 25 minutes, stirring frequently.
3. Stir in butter, molasses, salt, and ginger.
4. Pour into a greased 1½-quart baking dish. Pour the 1 cup cold milk over pudding.
5. Set in a baking pan. Pour boiling water around dish to within 1 inch of top.
6. Bake, covered, at 300°F about 2 hours. Remove cover and bake an additional 1 hour. Serve warm or cold with **cream** or **ice cream.**

6 servings

Bread Pudding

1 cup raisins
½ cup sherry
8 slices white bread
 Butter
4 eggs
½ cup sugar
 Dash salt
1 quart half-and-half
1½ teaspoons vanilla extract

1. Soak raisins in sherry 2 hours, stirring occasionally.
2. Trim crusts from bread and spread with butter. Place bread, buttered side down, in a 2½-quart casserole or soufflé dish.
3. Drain raisins and sprinkle over bread.
4. Beat remaining ingredients together. Pour over bread and let stand 30 minutes. Sprinkle with **cinnamon.**
5. Bake, covered, at 350°F 30 minutes. Remove cover and bake an additional 30 minutes, or until set.

8 servings

Peach Meringue Pudding

2 cans (21 ounces each) peach pie
 filling
¼ cup butter or margarine, melted
½ teaspoon cinnamon
⅛ teaspoon nutmeg
⅛ teaspoon allspice
½ cup slivered almonds
3 egg whites
½ cup sugar

1. Combine peach pie filling, butter, cinnamon, nutmeg, allspice, and almonds. Put into a 1½-quart casserole.
2. Bake, uncovered, at 350°F 30 minutes, or until bubbly. Remove from oven.
3. Beat egg whites until stiff, but not dry. Gradually beat in sugar until glossy. Evenly spread over hot peaches. Sprinkle with **cinnamon.**
4. Bake an additional 12 to 15 minutes, or until lightly browned.

6 servings

Apple Cream

6 cups sliced apples (about 2 pounds)
½ cup sugar
1 teaspoon cinnamon
1 teaspoon nutmeg
¼ cup butter or margarine
⅔ cup sugar
1 egg
½ cup flour
½ teaspoon baking powder
½ teaspoon salt
1 cup whipping cream

1. Toss the apple slices with a mixture of the ½ cup sugar, cinnamon, and nutmeg. Spread evenly in bottom of a buttered 9-inch square baking dish.
2. Cream together butter and ⅔ cup sugar. Add egg and continue beating until mixture is light and fluffy.
3. Blend flour, baking powder, and salt; beat into creamed mixture until just blended. Spread evenly over apples.
4. Bake, uncovered, at 350°F 30 minutes. Pour cream over surface and bake an additional 10 minutes, or until topping is golden brown. Serve warm with cream, if desired.

8 servings

Favorite Apple Pudding

6 or 7 medium firm, tart cooking apples, quartered, cored, pared, and cut in ⅛-inch slices
¾ cup firmly packed brown sugar
3 tablespoons flour
½ teaspoon salt
1 teaspoon cinnamon
¼ teaspoon nutmeg
3 tablespoons butter or margarine
1 teaspoon grated orange peel
¾ cup (3 ounces) shredded Cheddar cheese
5 slices white bread, toasted, buttered on both sides and cut in halves
¼ cup orange juice
½ cup buttered soft bread cubes

1. Arrange one third of the apple slices on bottom of a greased 2-quart casserole.
2. Thoroughly blend brown sugar, flour, salt, cinnamon, and nutmeg. Using a pastry blender or 2 knives, cut in butter and grated orange peel until mixture is in coarse crumbs. Mix in cheese.
3. Sprinkle one third of the sugar-cheese mixture over apples and cover with one half of the toast. Repeat layers. Cover the top with remaining apples and sugar-cheese mixture.
4. Pour orange juice over surface and top with the buttered bread cubes.
5. Bake, covered, at 425°F 30 minutes. Remove cover and bake an additional 10 minutes.

6 to 8 servings

Baked Apricot Pudding

1 tablespoon confectioners' sugar
1¼ cups (about 6 ounces) dried apricots
1 cup water
1½ tablespoons butter or margarine
1½ tablespoons flour
¾ cup milk
4 egg yolks
½ teaspoon vanilla extract
4 egg whites
6 tablespoons granulated sugar
Whipped cream

1. Lightly butter bottom of a 1½-quart casserole and sift confectioners' sugar over it.
2. Put apricots and water into a saucepan. Cover; simmer 20 to 30 minutes, or until apricots are plump and tender. Force apricots through a coarse sieve or food mill (makes about ¾ cup purée).
3. Heat butter in saucepan. Stir in flour. Gradually add milk, stirring until thickened and smooth. Remove from heat.
4. Beat egg yolks and vanilla extract together until mixture is thick and lemon colored. Spoon sauce gradually into beaten egg yolks while beating vigorously. Blend in apricot purée.
5. Using clean beater, beat egg whites until frothy. Add sugar gradually, beating constantly. Continue beating until rounded peaks are formed. Spread apricot mixture gently over beaten egg whites and fold until thoroughly blended. Turn mixture into prepared casserole. Set casserole in a pan of very hot water.
6. Bake, uncovered, at 350°F 50 minutes, or until a knife inserted halfway between center and edge comes out clean. Cool slightly before serving. Top with whipped cream.

6 servings

Baked Apple and Cheese Dessert

5 cups sliced apples (about 5 medium)
¾ cup firmly packed brown sugar
1 tablespoon lemon juice
½ cup flour
¼ teaspoon salt
½ teaspoon cinnamon
¼ teaspoon mace
¼ cup butter or margarine
1 cup (4 ounces) shredded sharp
    Cheddar cheese

1. Arrange apples in a 1½-quart shallow baking dish. Sprinkle with ¼ cup brown sugar and lemon juice.
2. Blend together remaining ½ cup brown sugar, flour, salt, cinnamon, and mace. Cut in butter until mixture is crumbly; mix in cheese. Spoon mixture over apples.
3. Bake, uncovered, at 350°F 30 minutes, or until apples are tender. Serve warm with **half-and-half.**

6 servings

Chocolate Custard

1 package (6 ounces) semisweet
    chocolate pieces
3 tablespoons half-and-half
3 cups milk
3 eggs
1 teaspoon vanilla extract
⅓ cup sugar
¼ teaspoon salt

1. Melt 2/3 cup chocolate pieces with half-and-half in top of a double boiler over hot (not boiling) water. Stir until smooth; spoon about 1 tablespoon into each of 8 custard cups or 10 soufflé dishes. Spread evenly. Put cups into a shallow pan; set aside.
2. Scald milk. Melt remaining 1/3 cup chocolate pieces and, adding gradually, stir in scalded milk until blended.
3. Beat together eggs, vanilla extract, sugar, and salt. Gradually add milk mixture, stirring constantly. Pour into chocolate-lined cups.
4. Set pan with filled cups on oven rack and pour boiling water into pan to a depth of 1 inch.
5. Bake, uncovered, at 325°F 25 minutes, or until a knife inserted halfway between center and edge comes out clean.
6. Set cups on wire rack to cool slightly. Refrigerate and serve when thoroughly cooled. Unmold and, if desired, garnish with whipped cream rosettes.

8 to 10 servings

Brazilian Pudim Moka with Chocolate Sauce

3 cups milk
1 cup half-and-half
5 tablespoons instant coffee
2 teaspoons grated orange peel
4 eggs
1 egg yolk
½ cup sugar
½ teaspoon salt
1 teaspoon vanilla extract
  Nutmeg
  Chocolate sauce
  Chopped Brazil nuts

1. Combine milk and half-and-half in top of a double boiler and heat over simmering water until scalded.
2. Add instant coffee and orange peel, stirring until coffee is dissolved. Remove from simmering water and set aside to cool (about 10 minutes).
3. Beat together eggs and egg yolk slightly. Blend in sugar and salt.
4. Gradually add coffee mixture, stirring constantly. Mix in vanilla extract. Strain through a fine sieve into eight 6-ounce custard cups. Sprinkle with nutmeg. Set cups in pan of hot water.
5. Bake, uncovered, at 325°F 25 to 30 minutes, or until a knife inserted in center of custard comes out clean.
6. Cool and chill. To serve, invert onto serving plates. Pour chocolate sauce over top and sprinkle with Brazil nuts.

8 servings

INDEX